HOW WE KILLED GOD

First published in 2017 by
CURRACH PRESS
23 Merrion Square
Dublin 2, Ireland
www.columba.ie

ISBN: 978 1 78218 330 3

Set in PT Serif 9.5/14
Cover design by Alba Esteban | Columba Press
Book design by Cathal Cudden | Bright Idea
Cover image by Chai Brady

Printed by Walsh Colour Print, Ireland

DAVID QUINN

HOW WE KILLED GOD

...and other tales of modern Ireland

CURRACH
PRESS

This book is dedicated to the memory of my friend and colleague, Tom O'Gorman, who died in tragic circumstances in 2014.

CONTENTS

ACKNOWLEDGEMENTS

I am grateful to those who have helped to contribute to this book in various ways, meaning all those who have been there in the 23 years that I have been writing a national newspaper column.

I am grateful to Damien Kiberd, who gave me my start at the *Sunday Business Post* in 1993, and to the various editors and other journalists I have worked with at *The Sunday Times*, *The Irish Independent*, and, of course, *The Irish Catholic*, which I edited for more than six years and to which I still contribute. I am grateful to the present editor, Michael Kelly, for his assistance in preparing this book, and to Garry O'Sullivan, Managing Director of Grace Communications, and to the staff at Currach Press, including the Managing Editor, Mags Gargan; the Editorial Assistant, Emilie Condron and Head Designer, Alba Esteban.

I would also like to thank *The Sunday Business Post*, *Sunday Times*, *Irish Independent* and *The Irish Catholic* for permission to reprint these columns.

Finally, I would like to thank my wife, Rachael, for her help and support down all the years.

FOREWORD

Quinn is a rare one, I tell you

by John Waters

A house next door to ours is called Iona, like the doughty band of 'anti-social-justice warriors' (aSJWs) headed up by David Quinn. In a country already post-fact, post-sense and post-meaning, the mere proximity of the house is a minor inconvenience for the SJWs who nightly prowl the sewer that is Twitter in search of characters to assassinate, so from time to time it is announced that I live in a house called Iona, which, they wrongly assert, is named after The Iona Institute. This is not intended as a merely interesting particular concerning my place of residence, but as an *incriminating fact*.

If I had my way, the building I live in would actually be called Iona. In my book, being associated with David Quinn and his band at Iona is a badge of honour, which I wear with pride. In a time when my phone rings a lot less than it used to, I am happy that among the consequences, one is that I *have* more time to talk to Quinn when he calls. We don't always agree – that's why they have both chocolate and vanilla, and also why our conversations tend to go on for so long.

Quinn is a rare one, I tell you. Not just a warrior but a chronicler too; he insists on describing the madness of our times in clear sentences as though for witnesses not yet born. In a country in which the fingers of one hand are sufficient to count the ranks of the remaining true newspapermen, he has remained steadfastly at his post when others, including myself, have long thrown our hats at it. He is forthright and brave and clear-minded and sensible. Decried and abused by sneaks and cowards, he has more bottle than the Guinness brewery and more smarties than Nestlé. So, in a lifetime or so, when our great-grandchildren sit around trying to figure out what madness befell our country in the early decades of the 21st Century, Quinn's witness to events and the connections between them will be up there among their most reliable guide to the truth. I promise it.

He is best known as a religious and social affairs commentator and his columns reflect this. He writes mostly about the most fundamental issues facing our society and each of its members: marriage, family, parenthood, education, healthy sexuality, and the story of Christ where it belongs: at the centre of human history. His persistent attention to these themes speaks about their importance.

It is above all his unerring instinct for cant and nonsense that leads him back again and again to these themes, just as his diviner's nose for the truth gets him hammered by agents of lies. He may disagree with me, but I do not see Quinn as a 'traditionalist', or even as a 'conservative' – bogey terms that have been booby-trapped by the twisters of things, so as to disqualify an opinion before it exits the speaker's mouth; I see him, rather, as a radical in pursuit of common sense, a teller of true stories.

The late writer and reluctant politician Vaclav Havel, writing about his observations of totalitarianism in his native Czechoslovakia, spoke of the deep nature of the 'nihilisation' that laid waste to his country, arising from ideologies that laid claim to having understood history completely. In such a process, history, past and future, is appropriated in a manner that eliminates the human element, the human story. All the unpredictability and possibility that arises from the human capacity for endless variety are removed and replaced with a sense that the future is simply an ideological continuum from the past, and that all that is required of the citizen, the human person, is to move forward into a utopia that has been prepared according to the diktats of history. Is this beginning to sound familiar? If not, you must have been away. This is the territory David Quinn prowls with his eagle eye and his nose for bad stuff. In a society in which the same twisted view of humanity is peddled not just by SJWs, but by the occupiers of the highest offices of government, the word 'totalitarian' is not too strong to describe what is happening to us.

The process, wrote Havel, begins with the commandeering of meaning by a single viewpoint, which is then made absolute, enabling history to be reduced to that single aspect. This occurs when the 'story' – that which gives human history its shape and meaning and structure – is eliminated from human culture. Everything becomes predictable, formulaic. And then: "Since the mystery in a story is the articulated mystery of man, his story began to lose its human content. The uniqueness of the human creature became a mere embellishment on the laws of history, and the tension and thrill in real events were dismissed as accidental and therefore unworthy of the attention of scholarship. History became boredom."

The comparison is not misplaced or disproportionate. What David Quinn also fights for is the right of men and women to live lives by their own lights, according to their given natures and infinite desiring. But we live in ominous times for human beings seeking to adhere to the truth and the givenness of things. Few of us, even in our most dystopian nightmares, anticipated the craziness that has descended upon Ireland in the past handful of years, and something tells me that the worst is yet to come.

I do not say that Quinn is our Havel; I say that for the needs of this moment he is as suited to our predicament as was Havel to that of his own country in the darkest days of the last century. He is our Mighty Quinn, and I am proud to call him my friend.

INTRODUCTION

David Quinn in conversation
with Michael Kelly

This book is named *How we killed God* because David feels God has been banished from both private and public life as "a relic of a more primitive age".

"Official Ireland has banished him from view almost completely. Many people have done the same thing in their own lives and for the same reasons. God became for them a symbol of the word 'no' and people don't want to hear that word in their lives," he says.

"Many others who still believe in God and want him to be part of their lives want to reduce him to the role of a servant of their wishes. He's good to turn to when you're in trouble, but he's basically there to smooth the path for you, to affirm you and give you a pat on the back for your efforts. He is not there to challenge you to greater things, never mind be a judge."

It was Nietzsche who told of a madman who ran through the town saying, 'God is dead and we have killed him'. For David this 'we' includes the Church itself.

"The Church could be tremendously authoritarian. If God in many people's minds represents the word 'no', it's because the Church has often presented him that way. And this is without even mentioning the hugely harmful effects of the scandals."

He thinks that the disaster for the Church, and for society, is that when people think of the word 'Church', they think of the institution, of the bishops and the priests and the religious. "This would be a bit like thinking of the FAI when you think of soccer. They don't think of Jesus and all the people making a genuine effort to follow him," he says.

"So, the Church has also helped to 'kill' God and eliminate him from view. Except you can't really 'kill' God, of course, you can only pretend he doesn't exist and that he doesn't matter. The task before all Christians now is to make him visible again."

One thing that belief in God sustains is the belief that we are all created equal in dignity and moral worth, and David is not convinced this can survive the 'death' of God over the long term. "Evolution on its own suggests the opposite; that we are radically unequal. Many of the critics of Christianity believe we are of equal dignity and moral worth without being able to give this a proper philosophical justification. They just assume it, without realising they assume it because 2,000 years of Christianity has made it seem self-evident. It is not self-evident at all."

In his more than 20 years as one of Ireland's most controversial newspaper columnists, David has been charting the marginalisation of God and religion in Irish life. He has been a ready champion for causes that he is passionate about and has been willing to step forward to put an argument where others have feared to tread.

In the unreal world of social media, Quinn is regularly subject to online tirades of abuse that would leave a lesser man shaken. In the political world, Quinn is a formidable opponent. His strategising around key issues and his sheer ability to make a logical argument make him a voice that his detractors cannot easily dismiss.

While he would be seen as one of the staunchest defenders of Catholicism in Ireland, he has not been shy about denouncing corruption in the Church where it has been exposed. When it came to the clerical abuse crisis, he was one of the first commentators out of the traps to insist that the Church must listen to those who have suffered and work to bring healing and compensation for the pain caused. He went so far as to call for heads to roll when senior prelates were shown to have been lax in their handling of abuse allegations. "Big deal", some might say. But, from one of the more-respected voices speaking from within the Catholic tradition, Quinn's interventions were a big deal.

So, where did it all start? Who is David Quinn? Journalism is in his DNA. "I'm the son and grandson of a journalist – professionally that's who I am.

"Personally, I am Northside Dubliner from a middle-class background, Vincentian-educated at St Paul's College, Raheny, and a business studies graduate from Dublin City University.

"I'm also a Catholic. A father and a husband," he says. Oddly for a man so much in the public eye, Quinn seems unaccustomed to talking about himself. "There's no kind of hidden depths or mysteries here," he tells me, "what you see is what you get."

"I can't offer any profound answers to what I am," he says.

And from where does the instinctive desire to jump in to the heart of a debate arise, I wonder.

"Well, I like standing up for what I think is right. Obviously, people sometimes stand up for things that are wrong, but they believe they are right. You're sometimes going to be wrong. But you have a duty to stand up for what you think is right," he says.

That fundamental belief in standing up for what he believes to be right seems to be a huge driving force for Quinn. When in the summer of 2017, columnist Kevin Myers lost his job after being accused of writing comments that were anti-Semitic in an article in *The Sunday Times*, he had few friends. Many journalists – perhaps keen to settle a score with the pugnacious Myers – sensed a feeding frenzy and joined in the calls for his removal.

Quinn resisted the temptation to run with the crowd and took the un-enviable role of trying to articulate a *via media*.

At the time of this interview, the controversy is still fresh. Quinn takes up the story: "Kevin Myers was accused of one thing he isn't, which is anti-Semitic, so the charge was absolutely unjust, and he was sacked for that.

"He wasn't sacked because of sexism or misogyny, but sacked because of a very clumsy comment that could reasonably be interpreted as anti-Semitic but should have been judged against his total record.

"His total record was absolute opposition to anti-Semitism," Quinn insists.

Like so much else in his career, Quinn has a visceral dislike for what he interprets as groupthink. So, Kevin Myers? "When you see a mob coming for somebody and then you see them dancing on his grave, and the completely disedifying sight of journalists and politicians dancing on the grave of journalists, I just thought that was appalling. And so, when I see that happening, I go out and defend that person, even if they wouldn't defend me in the future.

"I think that if you're in journalism or column-writing and commentating, and seeking popularity, you're in the wrong game," he says.

It's an admirable – some would say risky – stance to take at a time when many journalists are accused of following the maxim that he who pays the piper calls the tune.

For a man who has spent most of his life as a professional journalist, I wonder if Quinn has strong opinions on the profession he's a member of. His answer is swift, "there's far too much virtue-signalling going on among some journalists to be honest," by which he means a tendency for columnists to attach themselves to popular causes in a bid to appear relevant, modern and virtuous.

For Quinn, there's no courage in running with a herd. "This virtue-signalling is really safe. Now, people join mobs – commentators join mobs – to virtue signal and I just think this is the antithesis of good commentary. You should never ever join a mob, even if you agree with it; you shouldn't engage with mob behaviour and you shouldn't be looking to deprive people of their livelihoods.

"Journalists should be deprived of their livelihood if they're incompetent, if they've plagiarised, if they've falsified some story. They're the sort of things that ought to get a journalist sacked," according to Quinn. His obvious enthusiasm for quality journalism is evident. He credits his upbringing for this. Was his childhood one of lively debate with his journalistic father? "Not really," Quinn says, "but it was a home of newspapers."

He recalls that the family "used to get in about three or four newspapers every single day, and on a Sunday, seven newspapers would come into the house.

"I have three siblings, and I was the only one out of the four of us who was strongly interested in current affairs, and I developed this interest by the age of 12. It was partly because of all the newspapers that were coming into the house".

For Quinn, looking abroad has always provided a relief when Ireland seems suffocated by uniformity. "It so happens that one of the reasons why I was able to break away from the Irish consensus is that English newspapers were coming into the house that had different opinions about certain issues compared with the Irish papers".

So, what was the burning political issue that occupied a teenage David Quinn? "My big interest when I was a teenager was the Cold War. This was the era of Ronald Reagan and Margaret Thatcher." This was an issue where he first detected a tendency towards insularism in the Irish media. "Irish newspapers were mostly anti-Reagan and were quite sympathetic to an anti-American trope in the Cold War.

"Some of the big English newspapers were more likely to be pro-American, pro-NATO," he recalls. "They showed me that there was another way to think about those issues. Partly these newspapers coming into my house growing up rescued me from the Irish consensus".

As well as hostile voices towards religion, Quinn has often provoked the ire of liberal Catholics keen to see the Church abandon its more controversial teachings. He is unapologetic.

"I would call myself an orthodox Catholic, I wouldn't shy away from that label in the least, even though it's an obviously unfashionable kind of label."

Despite this, he would not describe himself as having a conservative Catholic upbringing: "It was more a political and Fine Gael upbringing."

"My father was editor of the *Evening Herald* for a few years (1969-1975) and worked for independent newspapers from the late 1940s until the late 1980s. His father before him worked for *The Clare Champion* and then transferred to the *Irish Independent* as its first ever political correspondent."

David recalls that his journalist grandfather had an armchair seat for some of the seminal events in modern Irish history. "He covered the War of Independence, the Treaty negotiations, the Civil War – he knew all the major players like Michael Collins and Éamon de Valera." David's grandfather met the ill-fated Collins the night before he was shot dead at Béal na Bláth. But, far from a dispassionate observer of such historic events, he used to use his press pass during the War of Independence to run messages for Collins. "So, that's my family background. I grew up in a very political house and a very Fine Gael house," he says.

Religiously, the family seem unremarkable. "My father would have gone to Mass, but I didn't see much evidence of religiosity on his part aside from that.

"My mother would have had a country piety and she would have said grace before meals, the Angelus, her prayers at bedtime. She didn't go off to prayer groups and we didn't have any holy pictures on the wall, or holy water when you came in the door or a sacred heart lamp in the house – we had nothing like that at all. And in fact, I remember after a while she stopped trying to get us to say grace before meals because we told her it was 'boring'. My poor mother.

"I went to Mass, but it wasn't an overly-religious household at all, it would have been conventionally religious."

If his father contributed to his political formation, his mother certainly contributed to what we might call his human formation. David recalls his mother as a quiet lady. "Her influence would have been at a kind of more personal level.

"She led by example. She was very unselfish," he says.

As a young adult, questions of religion didn't particularly interest Quinn.

"Politics was much more interesting to me than religion in those years, and that persisted through university as well. I would have been involved in many political debates, especially those to do with the Cold War. I hardly ever got involved in any debates about religion.

"Through school, I would have kept going to Mass and through university I kept going to Mass," he says. However, it was when he moved to Australia in 1986 that David stopped practising his faith. "I stopped going to Mass for a while, but it wasn't out of any sense of rebellion, it was out of pure laziness. I just wasn't motivated enough to go."

The Ireland of 1986 that Quinn left was a bleak place. Employment prospects were low – even for university graduates. "I remember," Quinn recalls, "one of the best jobs a classmate got was selling Mars food products around the country, and the reason this was a great job is because he had a company car. I was thinking, 'no, I'm not going to hang around. I'm getting out of the country'.

"A lot of graduates were going to America or England but I somehow took a fancy to going to Australia. I wanted to go somewhere different," he says.

David, along with a classmate, arrived in Sydney on December 1, 1986, at the height of the Australian summer. "It was so different to anything that I had ever experienced before.

"When you're in university - especially when you're living at home - even though you might leave university at the age of 22 or 23, you're in a kind of arrested adolescence. During the first six months in Australia, I did more growing up than in the previous six years."

Quinn believes that the best thing he ever did was go to Australia for those years.

He started out working for a market research company in Sydney before getting a job with an insurance company where he worked for five years.

"In Australia, my interest in religion was piqued, which is a bit surprising because when Irish people go abroad the opposite usually happens," he says.

The catalyst that caused him to re-think his Catholicism came from what might seem an unlikely source. "I met the woman who was to become my wife and she was from a Baptist background. I met her parents who were very devoutly Christian and took their faith very seriously." Quinn recalls being impressed by what he described as "a very authentic non-holy Joe" kind of belief.

As Protestants, their faith was very obviously differently expressed to Catholicism. There were none of the kinds of traditional devotional life of Catholics, the reformed churches being much more Bible-based.

It's often said that it's the example of people authentically living in a Christian way that attracts people, and this was certainly true for Quinn as he got to know this small community of Baptist believers.

"Quite a few members of this church were living not a million miles away from what is described in the Acts of the Apostles, and I had never seen this before, this strongly authentic Christian living. This impressed me and got me thinking."

Quinn recalls his reasoning at the time. "Basically, I had three choices, as I saw it. Am I secular in my basic outlook on life? I hadn't thought that through properly as I was always thinking politically rather than philosophically. And then, if I'm not secular, what is my religion? If it's Christian, should I be a Catholic or a Protestant in my basic outlook?"

He came very close to converting to Protestantism, "but in the end, I decided to find out what my side of the fence - so to speak - believed, and discovered to my surprise that Catholicism was far more rational than its critics would have us believe."

So, what of his religious education? The fourteen years spent in Catholic schools being formed in the faith? David is characteristically frank. "It was inadequate – I don't want to blame my school because my school was a perfectly good school, it was like probably every other school and maybe most schools to this day. It kind of took it for granted that you would absorb the faith by osmosis and it didn't think that it needed to go back to first principles and actually provide the building blocks of rational faith."

But for Quinn, faith is more than a rational way of living. "Christian faith is ultimately about a personal encounter with Christ, and if Christ is not at the centre of your Christian faith then you're not a Christian. The Baptists in Australia very much impressed that upon me; you must put Jesus at the centre of your faith. That's what Pope Benedict would always say: Christianity at its heart is a relationship. But, the rational side of it matters as well, and if there was no rational basis for it I could not be a Christian or a Catholic," he says.

People often look back at the 1979 visit of Pope St John Paul II to Ireland as a Catholic highpoint. Looking back, David remembers the time differently. "Catholic schools," he says, "basically took for granted that you would become Catholic through cultural osmosis. But when I was growing up in the seventies and eighties, that was already fading, certainly in Dublin, fading very badly.

"Too much of the Catholicism was based on conventional practice of the faith: you go to Mass, you say certain prayers, you might turn up at certain prayer groups, you might join the Legion of Mary or the Society of St Vincent de Paul," he says.

David is convinced that one of the Church's biggest failings is that Irish Catholics were never given an intellectual basis for their faith. "And so, when the questions came, nobody was equipped to answer them. And then, the poor hapless parents would get asked certain questions by their children and they wouldn't know how to answer, and the children would go away convinced that there were no answers."

David married Rachael in 1989. They tied the knot in a Protestant ceremony in a Protestant church. "If this might surprise some people," David says, "it is because there is a caricature around Catholics in general. Anybody who stands up for the Catholic faith immediately gets caricatured in a certain way. So, you mustn't like Protestants, you mustn't like atheists, you mustn't like anyone who has another point of view.

"The irony is that this caricature is itself a form of prejudice. It isn't alert to ecumenical trends in the Churches for example, even though these are decades old. Getting married in a Protestant church simply wasn't an issue for me."

While happy in Australia, David was always minded to return to Ireland and have a serious go at journalism. "The ink was in my veins," he recalls. Even though David's father discouraged him from following in his footsteps, his indulgence of David's love of current affairs eventually paved the way.

In Australia, before the internet, David kept abreast of things at home through regular newspaper clippings sent from his father. "I'd get a thick envelope once a fortnight and all these newspaper clippings would keep me up to date with what was happening in Ireland.

"A lot of the newspaper clippings consisted of the Catholic Church coming under attack, even though the scandals had not yet come to light. I noticed no one in the Irish media was offering a defence of Catholicism, except for the late Des Rush in the *Irish Independent* who was relegated to a side-strip column in the feature section every Saturday.

"So, I had in mind, when I go back, I'm going to try and offer a different point of view," he says. David quit his job in the insurance industry and he and his wife made plans to move to Ireland where Rachael hoped to find work as a nurse.

The couple made the move in 1993, and within 12 months, David had a weekly column in *The Sunday Business Post*. He is eternally grateful to the paper's then editor Damien Kiberd for giving him the break.

"The reason he [Kiberd] gave me my first break was because he himself knew there was a stifling consensus in Ireland. So, this stifling consensus didn't appear today or yesterday. He decided 'this Quinn guy is different'. At that point I'm young, I'm 31 years of age. So, I'm a young guy who is defending the Catholic point of view. This is novel and I quickly began to appear on radio and television because there was essentially no one else these shows could invite on with my point of view," he says.

But, before the regular column in *The Sunday Business Post*, David had been published in the now defunct *Sunday Press* newspaper. "I wrote an article and it was kind of abstract because it was saying that liberals tend to replace God with history. If you're on the 'wrong' side of history, you're equivalent to a sinner, and if you're on the 'right' side of history, you're equivalent to a saint.

"The editor of the *Sunday Press* at the time, admitted to me some years later that several journalists had come into his office after my article appeared and told him never to use me again. People would sometimes criticise me to Damien [Kiberd] as well, but he stood up to them. Damien himself would be mostly liberal on social issues, but simply did not like the media consensus," according to David.

In January 1994, he was offered the position of Editor of *The Irish Catholic* newspaper – a weekly newspaper that has been published since 1888.

It was a logical move, he recalls, "I had already nailed my colours to the mast in terms of what I believed."

David immediately set about placing the paper at the centre of debates and controversies involving the intersection between Church and State, or faith and culture.

"So, while some articles about issues like women priests or celibacy were carried, most opinion pieces would be about these points of tension between the Christian faith, the Catholic faith and the surrounding culture. These were often to do with the big social debates about divorce, the right-to-life, the proper relationship between Church and State, public funding of denominational schools and so on."

David's return to Ireland came just a year after Bishop Eamonn Casey sent shockwaves across the country when it was exposed he had secretly fathered a child.

Worse was to come. Punishing revelations about the Church's mishandling of allegations of abuse against priests were to dominate the first half of David's journalistic career.

"The cracks in the Catholic edifice had already appeared but the Brendan Smyth case was even more seismic," David recalls.

Smyth – a Norbertine monk – remains one of Ireland's most notorious abusers. The poor handling of an extradition request for Smyth to face charges in Northern Ireland by authorities in Dublin led to the collapse of the Fianna Fáil-Labour coalition in 1994.

At the same time, RTÉ had aired a one-hour documentary by Louis Lentin entitled *Dear Daughter*. In recounting the story of Christina Buckley, a woman's search for her parents, the film shed light on allegations of cruelty and abuse at Dublin's Goldenbridge Orphanage during the 1950s and 1960s when the institution was managed by the Sisters of Mercy.

David recalls that the film "broke the scandal of abuse in Church-run institutions. The Catholic Church rightly got roundly attacked over these things so I was writing and commenting on radio and television incredibly extensively on these scandals".

It was a difficult balancing act, maintaining the truths of the Catholic faith while being able to acknowledge and condemn the terrible wrongs that had been perpetrated against vulnerable children by people in the Church.

"In writing about the scandals, I had many concerns. One was that anyone in the Church responsible for these scandals ought to be held accountable. That meant bishops resigning, compensation being paid, offenders going to prison or forced out of ministry," he says.

Meanwhile, hapless Church leaders seemed incapable of comprehensively addressing the issue. "It was a source of endless frustration that the Church would not get ahead of the curve on this and reveal itself what had happened in all its dioceses and institutions. Instead we got a 'drip, drip, drip' of revelations dragged out of it bit by bit.

"We ended up with statutory inquiries, documentaries and so on instead of the Church getting everything out into the public domain itself.

"In 1996, the first child protection guidelines were issued by the

Church, the so-called 'Green Book'. I think it was the very month I became editor of *The Irish Catholic*."

"I remember writing some time later that as a goodwill gesture and to rebuild trust with the public, every bishop appointed before this date in 1996 ought to resign to rebuild the trust of the public.

"I remember being told by some clergy that this was incredibly naïve. Maybe it was, but my view was that when the public lose trust in the board of a company, the entire board would resign even though not every board member is equally guilty of causing whatever fault was found in the organisation. That never happened with the Catholic Church.

"If that had happened, and if the Church had got all the information out itself, no matter how damaging, it might have convinced some members of the public that the Church was taking the scandals seriously and not putting self-preservation first," he recalls.

As Editor of *The Irish Catholic*, David perceived that part of his role was to ensure that the essence of Catholicism was not disregarded in the rush to rightly expose the scandals. "Another side of my writing on this issue was to try and counter some of the anti-Catholic commentary attached to overall commentary on the scandals. For example, that the scandals were because of priestly celibacy. Or they were because of the male-only priesthood. Or because of the Church's teaching on human sexuality. Or because of its hierarchical nature. You would point out in response that other churches that don't have priestly celibacy and do have women priests have the same scandals and so do secular organisations. I would point this kind of thing out a lot but it was very hard to make people see this because they had no real points of comparison in this country, as the Catholic Church in Ireland was so dominant.

"The Church was an incredibly major part of civil society and it ran so much, often on behalf of the State. So, the industrial schools were run almost exclusively by the Catholic Church, whereas in other countries, the equivalent institutions would be run by Catholics, but also sometimes by Protestant organisations or by the state itself. So, in those countries you can make a readier comparison with non-Catholic institutions. This tends to show that there are no features intrinsic to Catholicism that cause these scandals in and of themselves," David believes.

What sort of effect did these revelations have on David's personal faith? Was he ever tempted to throw in the towel? His answer is an emphatic 'no'.

"My thinking has always been that even if 99.9% of the Christian population are hypocrites, it is still no excuse for you to be a hypocrite. What you've got to look at is the thing in itself and why should even the most appalling behaviour by Christians make you think that Jesus is not worth following, is not a good example of how to live?

"I hate sounding overly-pious, but at the centre of my mind is that Jesus remains Jesus, and God remains God.

"There is no organisation, no religion, no culture, no society, nothing comprised of human beings that does not have dark chapters. You can't point to anything, there is no idea that does not have dark chapters. The 20th Century is full of bad secular ideas, some of which killed millions of people. Think about the number of people killed in the 20th Century in the name of equality, in the attempt to create a classless society in the Soviet Union, for instance. But does this mean that the idea of equality is bad in itself? The answer is 'no'. The idea of equality is either a good or a bad idea on its own merits. So, I would take the same attitude towards Christianity," he says.

In 2003, David quit both *The Irish Catholic* and his weekly column in *The Sunday Times* to take up the prestigious post of Religious Affairs Correspondent with the country's biggest-selling daily newspaper, the *Irish Independent*.

"The scandals were still very much in the news and the *Irish Independent* figured it needed a specialist reporter. After all, the number of journalists specialising in religious affairs is tiny. So, they're thinking, 'who are we going to get?' There weren't too many alternatives!"

By 2005, David had itchy feet and wanted to realise an ambition that had been growing for a long time. He saw the need for an organisation, a think-tank that would provide research and commentary about the role of religion in society and in defence of the family. Thus, The Iona Institute was born.

Active for over a decade now, the organisation has contributed to public debates to a far greater extent than some much larger and more-established organisations.

The Iona Institute is part of a pattern across David's life that has seen him want to challenge what he sees as a consensus. "What I was noticing, in all the years as editor of *The Irish Catholic* and then working in the *Irish Independent*, was research coming into the newsdesk that would advance say, the pro-choice side of the argument, or the 'family-diversity' side of the argument, meaning those who think marriage is just one more option and not of special importance. So, I felt that what was needed was an organisation which would challenge this kind of thinking. I knew there was a lot of research saying marriage is very important and that it really matters for children, and that children really ought to have the involvement of both their mother and father in their lives assuming they are fit parents. I knew that all this research existed but it wasn't getting out there at all and, a story might break on various issues and a press release would come out and there was no press release coming from any organisation with a Christian or Catholic point of view. So, I said 'I'm going to set this up'.

"One of the main purposes of Iona's existence is to take part in media debates. Another thing, more minor, you'd see organisations commissioning opinion polls and finding out about public opinion on x, y or z. Now you can criticise opinion polls all you like in terms of the type of questions that get asked, but opinion polls do have their value. A recent example is the Good Friday drinking laws. Does the public believe these should be abolished? We commissioned a poll which discovered the public is split down the middle on it. No one else was going to commission that poll other than Iona. So that's the kind of thing I mean. These do help to inform debate a little bit. So that's why it was set up."

Iona remains a small organisation with David as Director and two other part-timers working in the office. "We are very small compared with our opposite numbers, but we have a good profile among people who pay attention to these things. I think our existence encourages people who share our point of view," he says.

But, David is also modest – perhaps realistic – about the impact of the Iona Institute. "Have we been able to turn the tide? No, because how do you do that? Where has this happened in the West? The cultural currents in the West are strongly running in the direction of the kind of hyper-individualism which emphasises the idea of personal choice above all else. So, it's a 'personal choice' to get an abortion, to choose assisted suicide, even the right to choose what sex or gender you are. Objective claims to truth, such as those made by Christianity, many people find deeply offensive.

"This kind of hyper-individualism leans towards a kind of relativism in areas of truth and morality. It's what the previous Pope [Benedict XVI] called a 'dictatorship of relativism'."

Perhaps for David personally and the Iona Institute as an organisation, the debate and referendum on same-sex marriage was the most prominent. But, he has no regrets. "A kind of consistent theme of my time as a columnist has been to step in where there appears to be no debate taking place.

"One of the reasons I set up Iona was to defend a particular conception of the family, which happens to be the Christian one as well. Now when I set up Iona, same-sex marriage was not even on the agenda. So, it wasn't with that in mind that I set it up, but I did think marriage was very important.

"Among the reasons that marriage is very important is because it gives a child the best chance of being raised by their own mother and father. So, it would have been to me an act of cowardice to stay out of the debate about same-sex marriage because what same-sex marriage did was it changed our total view of the family. It announces that actually you don't really need a mother and father, that two fathers or two mothers are just the same. Natural ties? They don't really matter because two men obviously can't both be the natural parents of the same child. To me, this was ridiculous because so many adopted children go looking for their parents, even if they were very well loved. Many, not all, go looking for natural parents.

"We see the popularity of programmes like 'Who do you think you are?' people trying to trace their family tree. So, in a country where our Irish names always mean 'son of' and 'daughter of', to assume that the natural ties to a parent don't matter is absurd. I thought same-sex marriage was an attack on the rights of a child so that's why I stepped up, and that was obviously incredibly challenging because you had all kinds of abuse hurled your way."

The debate on same-sex marriage raged for several years and culminated in the 2015 referendum to change the constitutional definition of marriage. The result was 62% in favour of same-sex marriage, while 38% - almost two in five people – opposed. "I and a handful of others who took part in that debate in a public way were proud to have represented almost 40% of the people, when no political party and no major media outlets would."

Even David's critics had to admire his role in the campaign. The *Irish Times* on the Monday after the referendum editorialised about the result and opined that, by and large, the 'no' side in the referendum ran a clean campaign.

The same editorial described David as "a model of grace in defeat".

"It was a graceful note on their part as well to say that, because obviously during the campaign we were getting huge abuse on social media. I basically stopped really looking at social media, there was just no point. Fortunately, it is the case, objectively speaking, that social media is not representative of the broader public."

David is clearly a practising Catholic, does he think of himself as a religious person? "That's a term that's full of baggage.

"I'm not going to describe myself as a spiritual person, because that's a cop-out term.

"So, am I a religious person? Well, I believe in God and I'm a Christian and I pray and I go to Mass. So, is my faith is important to me? Yes, it is."

Does David regret what Ireland has become? He is philosophical. "Yes and no. The Church was too authoritarian in the past and there had to be a move towards more personal freedom. But it has sometimes come at the expense of other values, like the right-to-life, or marriage and the family. It's terrible to see so many fathers not helping to raise their own children. There is also a lot of anti-Catholicism now. Let me define what I mean by that: you take someone like Nigel Farage of the United Kingdom Independence Party. Everyone would agree that he's anti-EU. If you take the far-left parties, everyone would readily agree they are anti-Labour, anti-Fine Gael, anti-Fianna Fáil. Now, why do we say this? Because their criticism of the things they dislike is constant, because they put the worst interpretation on everything these organisations do and they never give them the benefit of the doubt. Only their 'sins' are highlighted, and they give them credit for nothing.

"The scandals were terrible beyond belief, but they are no more the essence of Catholicism than acts of terrorism carried out in the name of Islam are the essence of Islam.

"Anti-Catholicism has taken the place of the anti-English feeling that existed here for a long time. You could put together a long and accurate charge sheet against England when you go back down the centuries. Ireland was mainly plundered and oppressed for most of the time we were under English rule, but our views about England are now more balanced. We know that the criticism of England is not the full story about England. England gave much to the world, for example parliamentary democracy; it has a long tradition of common law that's actually a very good tradition. It hasn't been susceptible to the kind of violent revolutions that have regularly happened on the continent and it stood alone against Hitler for a time in World War II at a crucial period.

"Therefore, the colonial history of Britain is not the full story any more than the oppressive behaviour and abuses of the Catholic Church are the whole story. Remember, whereas Britain mostly plundered this country, the Catholic Church did, and is doing, an awful lot of good here down the centuries. I hope eventually we get to a more balanced view of it."

And the bruised and battered Catholic Church in Ireland? Is David optimistic about the future? "I'd say a couple of things on that score: one is that the decline in vocations, Mass attendance and so on is a result not of secularism pure and simple, but of rising individualism.

"Political parties are being hurt by the same phenomenon. The membership of political parties compared with say the 1950s is far down, also voters tend to be on the older side; trade union memberships are declining rapidly and the members are older; newspaper readership is also declining and getting older. So, people don't tend to make the major kind of commitments that they used to make and marriage is also affected because now fewer than half the adult population is married.

"So, institutional belonging of various kinds is on the wane and not just religion. In other words, we need to look at the bigger picture and see how excessive individualism is harming the country as a whole.

"I also think it is a bad thing if people lose sight of the transcendent aspect of life. St Augustine's words are permanently true: 'we are made for you, O Lord, and our hearts are restless until they rest in you'. When people aren't looking for God directly, they will look for substitutes. The Celtic

Tiger was such a one. But what is really regrettable is that when many people think of the Church, they don't think of Jesus, they think of the institution. We need to change that. Even people who dislike the institution intensely tend to have a good opinion of Jesus."

Does David ever feel disheartened by some of the criticism he receives? It's water off a duck's back. "Let's not exaggerate," he laughs, "most people have never heard of me. I'm unpopular with people who don't like the Church. On the other hand, I get a lot of emails of support and phone calls of support and people sometimes stop me in the street and say, 'well done,' or 'keep up the good work'.

"When you stand up for something you will attract praise and criticism. Obviously, I go against the current secular consensus by and large, so I'm not going to win much support in fashionable quarters. So be it."

Michael Kelly is Consulting Editor with Columba Press.

CHAPTER 1

HIGH STAKES IN THE BATTLE FOR CATHOLICISM

1994

Fr Richard McBrien is chairman of the theology department at Notre Dame, the famous US Catholic university. Writing in Notre Dame's alumni magazine in 1987, he asked, in so many words, how Catholics were going to survive the present pontificate.

Given McBrien's portrait of Pope John Paul II, this will be a difficult task. As he tells us, in order to understand the present Pope, we must keep in mind that "Karol Wojtyla has known only two kinds of political regime in his adult life: Nazism and Communism", some of whose tactics he has learned only too well.

"Some have pointed out... that John Paul may, quite unwittingly, be imitating the political tactics of his erstwhile communist opponents: brook no dissent, place hardliners in positions of enforcement, make an example of those who deviate from the party line by punishment that is swift, firm and highly visible."

In his book, *No Lions in the Hierarchy*, Fr Joe Dunn concurs almost entirely with McBrien's opinion. This is not surprising, as this picture of the Pope has long since become an integral part of the canon of left-wing Catholic orthodoxy.

Dunn writes: "John Paul... has done a lot of harm to the Church in my generation. And most of the people whose opinion I value think more or less the same way..."

As it happens, all those people whose opinion he values belong to the Catholic left, and sometimes to the extreme left. In light of this it is hardly surprising that Dunn should have gained such an overwhelmingly negative impression of John Paul II.

Dunn may very well have read authors such as Michael Novak, Richard John Neuhaus, or Paul Johnson, all of whom view the Pope favourably, but his book provides no evidence of it. In more balanced works some effort at least is made to present a contrary opinion, if only to then reject it. Dunn is either unaware of what such a position might be, or he is as guilty as the Pope of suppressing those views with which he happens to disagree.

In the story of John Paul II and his critics as it is told by the left, dissidents are moderate but heroic folk who, against all the odds, are striving to promote more lay involvement in the Church, more participation in the Church's decision-making process, a stronger orientation towards the poor, and a more liberal attitude towards contraception, divorce, women priests, and sexual matters in general.

These dissidents occupy pride of place in Dunn's book. They are the 'lions' whose views he would presumably like to see reflected in the Church hierarchy. Among them are such luminaries as Leonardo Boff, Rosemary Radford Ruether, Bernard Haring, Charles Curran, Hans Kung, Albert Nolan, and Richard McCormick.

However, a deeper examination of the works of these same writers reveals that, in the main, while their proposals for the Church are ostensibly moderate they are in fact extremely radical. The implications of their proposals are so far-reaching that, if implemented, they would change Catholicism utterly.

Take, for example, Leonardo Boff. Boff was summoned to Rome some years ago for, in Dunn's words, "promoting a grassroots church, parallel to and opposed to the hierarchy. So Cardinal Arns and Cardinal Lorscheider... came to Rome to support him in his inquisition. So much for fears of him representing a parallel Church!"

What Dunn does not tell us is that Boff views the hierarchy as an integral part of the ruling class and therefore as an inherently oppressive structure. He believes that no teaching or directing authority must be allowed to come "from above", but instead must rise up from below. His views on how power and authority work in society and in the Church are, at the very least, quasi-Marxian and most definitely not Catholic.

On a visit to the USSR in 1987 Boff wrote that the Soviet Union was "a clean, healthy society". On another occasion he declared that he could detect the Holy Spirit working through the events of 1917.

Elsewhere, Dunn quotes Rosemary Bradford Ruether in the context of an attack on *Veritas Splendor.*

"We must recognise the crisis of a Church that has committed the ultimate error, the sin against the Holy Spirit, by refusing to stand under the judgement and grace of God as our ultimate hope..." Ruether is one of the most radical theologians operating today. She provides an excellent example of the way in which many theologians appropriate the language and symbols of Christianity, drain them of their historical meaning, and then reinvest them with entirely new meanings of their own.

When asked on one occasion why she remained in a Church she believed to be inherently, and not just accidentally, oppressive, Ruether replied: "You can't make a revolution without Xerox machines, and the Church has Xerox machines." In other words, the Catholic Church has resources as well as a recognised brand name which she and her colleagues wish to use for their own purposes.

Although she uses such words as 'God' and 'the Holy Spirit', she does not use them in a way that can by any stretch of the imagination be deemed Catholic or even Christian. According to her autobiographical essay, at the outset of her academic career she "discarded the doctrine of the personal immortality of the soul". She "crossed over" to "autonomous selfhood". She came to view dogmas not as statements of ontological truth, but merely as useful symbols. Ruether believes in a "god" who is to be found solely within each of us. She does not believe in the transcendent God of Judaeo-Christianity.

She is not alone in holding such beliefs. Thomas Sheehan of Loyola University, himself a member of Catholicism's left-wing intelligentsia, has written that most of today's "internationally recognised" theologians deny, among other things, that Mary was a virgin at Jesus' birth, deny that Jesus was divine, deny that he intended founding a church, or a priesthood, or a hierarchy, or that he rose from the dead. Once these beliefs are denied, there is little left which is uniquely Catholic.

In his book *Credo: the Apostles Creed Explained for Today*, Hans Kung, a leading light for liberal Catholics everywhere, in essence explains away the Creed and reduces it to little more than poetry. Kung would claim that he is attempting to make Christianity accessible to the modern person, but his 'cure' only serves to kill the patient.

In a review in *The Tablet* last year, Fr Gerard Collins opened with this comment: "A Jewish friend of mine who is currently reading his way through Kung's works recently said to me: 'But he doesn't accept the divinity of Jesus.' Kung's latest book will not help me to correct my friend's conclusion. Jesus comes across as the definitive prophet through whom God spoke and acted decisively and in a unique way, but not as God's self-gift in person."

In an irate reply, Kung informed readers that he was working on a book in which a "wide range of distinguished scholars defend the full Catholic orthodoxy of my theology". This sheds more light on the "distinguished scholars" in question than on Kung's "orthodoxy", and brings us back to the beliefs, or lack thereof, of Sheehan's "internationally recognised" theologians.

On this matter of theologians insisting on their right to be called 'Catholic', while at one and the same time denying the most basic and essential Catholic beliefs, Michael Dummett, Wykeham Professor of Logic at Oxford, and a convert to Catholicism has written: "What, without lack of charity, we may legitimately find astonishing is that people who have adopted positions which imply that from the very earliest times, the Catholic Church, claiming to have a mission from God to safeguard divinely revealed truth, has taught and insisted on the acceptance of falsehoods enshrined in her most sacred books, and is, accordingly, as much a fraud as her enemies have always maintained, should think it proper to teach such views to those in training for the priesthood. And indeed, their actions are helping to transform the Church into something distinctly fraudulent..."

He continues: "The monolith Church was never a reality and is not an ideal, but the divergence that now obtains between what the Catholic Church purports to believe and what large or important sections of it in fact believe, ought, in my view, be tolerated no longer: not if there is to be a rationale for belonging to that Church."

In much the same vein, Dr Anthony Kenny, a former priest and an agnostic, who is now Master of Balliol, Oxford, has written: "I am old-fashioned enough to believe that if the Church has been wrong on so many topics as forward-looking clergy believe, then her claims to impose belief and obedience on others are, in the form in which they have traditionally been made, mere impudence."

This Pope, or any Pope for that matter, is charged above all else with preserving the Faith as it has been transmitted to us over the centuries. The appointed task of the Pope and his bishops is the preservation of Catholicism as a meaningful and coherent idea. John Paul II is being unfairly pilloried for standing over and defending teachings which are the foundation of Catholicism. Indeed, it could well be argued that, given the threat to Catholicism posed by dissident theologians, the Pope has been remarkably restrained in his treatment of them. This certainly would seem to be the opinion of Professor Dummett.

The extent and scope of dissent today is possibly greater than at any other point in Church history. It is not restricted simply to matters such as divorce, women priests, or contraception. It reaches into and threatens the very core of Catholicism, and indeed of Christianity.

If theologians such as Boff or Ruether or Kung win the day, then Catholicism will simply cease to exist. All we will be left with will be the name and form and symbols of Catholicism.

None of this is drawn out in Fr Dunn's book. It thus gives us a very unbalanced impression of the state of the Church today, and it fails to tell us how high the stakes are in the battle for control of Catholicism.

TWO VIEWS OF MORALITY FIGHT IT OUT FOR THE CHURCH

1995

Note: This was written following the appearance of the late Cardinal Cahal Daly on the Late, Late Show, an appearance that caused much debate.

Am I the only one who thought it was the audience and not the cardinal which let itself down on *The Late Late Show* last Friday night? No account of the proceedings which I read seemed in the least taken aback by the ill-tempered behaviour of large sections of the audience. In fact, several commentators seemed almost to applaud the audience's behaviour.

One individual who was in the studio told me that the "hatred" displayed by some members of the audience towards what the cardinal represented was "palpable".

This doesn't surprise me. Divisions within the modern Church are deep and bitter, as deep and bitter as any which ever existed between old-time Trots and Stalinists.

What we have in the Church at present are two distinct factions with two quite irreconcilable views on authority and morality. One has in mind an 'open, democratic' Church, the other a hierarchical one.

One is relativistic in its approach to morality, the other absolutist. One is in lockstep with modern trends, the other in a head-on collision with them.

Take, by way of illustration, the issue of compassion. The accusation was flung about the studio with great abandon last Friday night that "the Church lacks compassion". People feel that the Church is not responding to their needs.

This is a very real and widespread perception. What is it based on? Surely it is not true that the Church is unavailable to people.

As the cardinal pointed out, there are numerous priests, nuns and lay people doing sterling work helping people in myriad ways. What then is the problem?

I think it is this: our perception of what constitutes compassion has radically altered. As our attitude towards morality has become more relativistic, we have become far more impatient at the Church telling us what is right and wrong. This is especially true in the area of so-called 'private' morality.

Since it is no longer perceived to be the business of the Church to 'stick its nose' into our private affairs, what it should instead be doing is assisting us in carrying out whatever plan of action we have already decided upon for ourselves.

The attitude of modern people then is that it is up to each of us to decide for ourselves what is right and wrong. Having done that, it is not for the Church to tell us our decision is wrong, rather it is for the Church to help us carry out our decision. If it refuses to do so because it thinks what we are doing is wrong, then *ipso facto* it is showing a lack of compassion.

In total contrast, orthodox Christians think compassion consists not of helping people to carry out their plan of action almost regardless, but rather in helping people in every way possible to do the right thing.

In a relativistic climate, pastoral work is extremely problematic for the priest, nun or layperson trying their best to teach what the Church teaches. In walks someone who is living with a person outside marriage. What do you do? Tell them as delicately as possible that the Church cannot condone what used to be called 'living in sin'? If you do, they'll likely walk straight back out the door again. In walks another person who is on the pill. A strict Catholic will have problems with this, but once again if you point out the Church's official teaching, you again run the risk of alienating the person who has come to you for help. What of the person who comes in contemplating an abortion? More of the same kind of problem.

In each case, if you try even obliquely to put across the Church's teaching, you are going to be accused of lacking compassion. This in fact is a very unfair criticism. No one can expect a person to cooperate in what they believe is wrongdoing.

Yet, if the Church insists on teaching right and wrong in its pastoral work, it runs the risk of alienating all those people who think it has no business teaching right and wrong, especially in the area of personal morality.

There are only two answers to this: adopt the liberal line and accept a relativistic view of morality, i.e. go with the flow; the second is to go all out in an effort to roll back the present relativistic climate, i.e. be counter-cultural.

There are no prizes for guessing which approach I favour. The Church must be true to itself and to what it sincerely believes to be true. It must hold true to its view of compassion and right and wrong. It must teach very clearly right from wrong and the do everything it possibly can to help people with the often onerous task of doing the right thing.

If the liberal approach was the way to popularity, then we would have a good reason to expect that the Anglican Church in England would be enjoying its greatest popularity ever. It has permitted artificial contraception since the 1930s. It is on the point of allowing divorced people to re-marry in church.

It allows women priests. It has a fairly liberal approach to abortion.

Is it well loved? Are people coming to Sunday service in droves? Are they banging on the priests' doors for pastoral advice? No. In terms of regular attendance, the Anglican Church is at its lowest ebb ever.

Hardly anyone pays it the slightest bit of attention. It has almost nothing to say which people can't hear louder and clearer from secular sources.

The task of the Church is to do a much better job communicating its core message.

If people think the Church is irrelevant now, they will doubly think so if it follows the Anglican route.

One way or another, the Church has no business whatsoever listening to people who have successfully confused the spirit of Vatican II with the spirit of the age.

CHAPTER 3

ON THE PRIVATE LIVES OF OUR POLITICIANS

1998

Ireland is in a very smug, complacent mood right now. The economy is roaring, a cultural revival is catching the attention of the world and, best of all, the Irish can look down their noses at the mighty United States. While America works itself into a paroxysm over Bill and Monica, Ireland is taking Bertie and Celia in its stride.

Who would have believed it? Catholic Ireland is now more easy-going about the private lives of its politicians than Britain or America. The sight of Bertie Ahern strolling along the Great Wall of China accompanied by a woman to whom he is not married causes hardly a ripple. A few phone calls here, a couple of letters there and that's about it.

It's quite a change and one worth contemplating. How can it be that holy, Catholic Ireland has suddenly become so tolerant of what liberals coyly term 'non-traditional' family forms? Is this apparent tolerance a sign that Ireland is indeed becoming the more pluralist and inclusive place about which we hear so much, or is the true explanation altogether more complex and more interesting?

I think the latter.

Consider this: taken as a whole Britain remains a more liberal society than Ireland. Yet when Robin Cook, the foreign secretary, left his wife for his lover, we are told that Downing Street forced him to choose between the two. He had to return to one or marry the other. He could not have it both ways.

Greece is almost certainly a less liberal society than Ireland and far less liberal than Britain, but when the then-prime minister Andreas Papandreou publicly humiliated his wife by leaving her for a much younger, more glamorous woman, there was an initial furore. Then the Greek electorate voted him back into office all the same.

Papandreou married Mimi, it is true, but he was not faced with a Robin Cook-style ultimatum. He did it more or less in his own time. This traditional society was altogether more tolerant and forgiving than cool Britannia.

Maybe the explanation for this apparent paradox is the fairly mundane and commonplace one that Mediterranean and Catholic societies are more easy-going about these things than their more puritanical counterparts. In other words, a society's tolerance of human frailty has little to do with liberalism as such and a whole lot more to do with the religious character of a people. Britain may be more secular than either Ireland or Greece but a residue of the old puritanism remains. The same goes for America.

In the case of Ireland, however, I suspect that this goes only part of the way towards explaining the tolerance shown to Ahern and Celia Larkin. While it is true that Catholicism in general has never been as puritanical as some varieties of Protestantism, Irish Catholicism has traditionally been regarded as more ferocious and less tolerant than continental Catholicism.

A fuller explanation is perhaps that Ireland is becoming more liberal and Irish Catholicism is becoming more continental. Maybe, in this respect anyway, the Irish are getting more like the Greeks or Italians and less like the British or Americans. Another factor is the attitude of the media. The Irish media are peopled almost entirely by liberals of one kind or another. Liberals make a much sharper distinction between the private and the public than conservatives.

Downing Street's ultimatum to Cook was almost certainly delivered out of fear of a backlash from the Tory press. No newspaper in Ireland would behave in such a way. More likely they would argue that if Ahern and Larkin's relationship is having any effect at all on public opinion then it is probably to the good because it is encouraging the Irish public to be more tolerant of diverse family forms. No conservative paper would ever run a line like this.

One more explanation might be Ireland's ambivalent attitude towards divorce. Remember that the divorce amendment was passed in 1995 by a margin of just 0.6%. Which would the Irish people prefer: a divorced taoiseach or what we have at present? In another country where divorce is more commonplace, maybe Ahern would have remarried by now. Who can say?

All in all, the pubic tolerance shown to Ahern and Larkin seems to be the result of a combination of factors: Ireland is becoming more liberal; it does not have a heritage of puritanism; the media are uniformly liberal in outlook; there is an ambivalent attitude towards divorce.

What I am writing about here is an extremely sensitive issue. The silence surrounding it is almost deafening. The Irish public is like the dog that did not bark.

My own interest in it is not to comment on the relationship between Ahern and Larkin as such, but to try to explain why the dog is not barking. The reaction is a phenomenon well worth exploring because it says so much about the kind of society Ireland is becoming. What does bother me about that society is the peculiar sense of arrogance overtaking it. It is proud of its 'liberalism' in the same ugly, narrow way it was once proud of its Catholicism.

Not so long ago Ireland would cast its gaze across the Irish Sea to England, or across the Atlantic to America, and feel both envious and morally superior at the same time. Ireland may have been poorer, but it was the land of saints and scholars.

Today when it looks across to Britain and America, the feeling of envy is gone, but the sense of moral superiority remains. Instead of feeling more Catholic, Ireland feels more tolerant and mature and progressive. The reaction to Ahern and Larkin say many things about the sort of society Ireland is in 1998, some good, some bad. One thing it tells us is that the old urge to feel morally superior to others is not yet gone. The more things change, the more they stay the same.

CHAPTER 4

TIME TO ATONE FOR CHILD ABUSE

1998

The Catholic Church in Ireland is haemorrhaging. It is losing members so fast that early in the next century it may find that Mass attendance has dropped to the average throughout the English-speaking world, that is 20% to 25% of 'Catholics'. It is losing its moral authority even more rapidly. There are a host of reasons for this. One is the continuing trail of clerical sex abuse cases passing through the courts and the public perception that the Church's response to these scandals has been wholly inadequate.

In its defence, the Church will say that it is being unfairly singled out, that other organisations have also had their share of child abuse scandals, and that incidence of clerical sex abuse is no higher among the clergy of other Churches.

It will further point out that it now has guidelines in place that lay out what must be done when such cases arise in the future. It will say that in the past, when cases of sexual abuse were brought to the attention of Church authorities, they acted according to the knowledge of the time. That is, they turned to psychiatrists who advised them that with appropriate treatment, the offender could be returned to normal pastoral ministry. They have issued one apology after another to the victims of abuse and to the wider community. They have offered help and counselling services to those same victims.

All this is true, but it cuts little ice with the public and none at all with the media. It sounds like special pleading. The apologies ring hollow, the expressions of pain seem insincere. The Church's reaction, its critics will say, was forced from it, and it would never have put on the sackcloth and ashes without the media exposing its shortcomings at every turn.

So, what is the Church to do? How can it convince a sceptical public of the sincerity of its feelings about this matter? It might try drawing a lesson from everyday life. Even at the most trivial level, when a person is sorry for some wrong they try to demonstrate the sincerity of their apology by backing it up with an appropriate deed, based on the timeless maxim that actions speak louder than words. The greater the wrong, the greater the act of reparation.

The Church's response to the child's sex abuse scandals has, to date, come nowhere near meeting the public's expectation. Whether it likes it or not, whether the public reaction is justified or not, that is the fact of it, and in this instance the public expectation is justified. It is justified because, as the public correctly senses, the scale of the wrong done by members of the Church to children in their care has not been backed up by an appropriate act of contrition (a Catholic term if there ever was one).

When a person enters the confessional and asks for forgiveness for sins committed, he or she must make an act of contrition and will be asked by the priest to perform some act of penance. What the Church asks of its members it should demand of itself.

The question is, what would amount to an appropriate act of contrition? What would be enough to convince the public?

Three possibilities come to mind. First of all, the Church should consider conducting an internal investigation into its handling of the clerical sex abuse cases. Any such inquiry should be led by an independent and trusted legal figure. The findings should be made public, and if heads must figuratively roll, as has happened in the case of the Irish Amateur Swimming Association, then so be it.

Second, it should consider laicising offending priests. Catholics who have an abortion, or who conduct abortions in full knowledge of what they are doing, incur the penalty of automatic excommunication from the clerical Church. Clerical sex offenders do not. This strikes the public as inconsistent.

If there is good reason for this seeming inconsistency, then it should be communicated to the public in a far better manner than has so far been the case.

Finally, it should consider selling off some of its property in order to set aside a fund of some kind for bona fide victims of abuse. There are any number of practical arguments against this – aren't there always? For instance, how can genuine claims be distinguished from false ones? Will it send the size of claims through the roof? Also, all property, even the almost empty seminaries, is being put to some use. If sold, it would have to be replaced.

The problem for the Catholic Church is that, as has happened elsewhere in the world, the scale of damages awarded against it might eventually force it to sell off property in any case. Better to do it now while there is still goodwill to be gained.

I have no doubt that even if these options are considered, all will be ruled out of court for all kinds of reasons. Fine. But the Church must know that it needs to do something radical. It needs to demonstrate to society the authenticity of its horror in the face of the worst scandals to have beset it in living memory. Can it really be beyond it to find the appropriate gesture?

In the end, the Church's credibility is on the line. Bishops know that when they speak out on some issue or another it is always in the shadow of the clerical abuse scandals. It needs to act, and it needs to act now.

CHAPTER 5

ARCHBISHOP COLLARED
BY THE SENSITIVITY POLICE

1999

There are few more terrifying sights in nature than a feminist pack with the smell of blood in its nostrils. No sooner had news broken that the Archbishop of Dublin, Desmond Connell, had put his foot in it over contraception than the pack could be heard howling at the moon.

Superintendents Mary Henry, Liz McManus, Noreen Byrne and Helen Keogh of the sensitivity police cried foul as they moved in with a warrant for the arrest of the hapless prelate on the grounds that he was being "insensitive". In the land of the therapeutic politics this was a serious crime.

His remarks were "insensitive in the extreme", said Senator Keogh. They were an "outrage", agreed Ms Byrne, commissar of the National Women's Council. "Eccentric and daft", charged new Labour recruit, Liz McManus. On *Prime Time* on Wednesday night Senator Henry oozed compassion from every pore as she sympathised with those couples hurt by the archbishop's comments. At one point she came tantalisingly close to becoming the first person in history to force her face into soft focus without the aid of trick photography.

Come to think of it, the level of outrage caused by Connell's remarks was on par with that caused by any given revelation from the tribunals on any one day. What can he have possibly said to compete so effectively in the Outrage Derby?

Last Tuesday night he delivered a talk at St Patrick's College, Maynooth, on the topic of *Humane Vitae*, the papal document which caused much furore in 1968 by reaffirming the Church's opposition to artificial contraception. During the talk he uttered the offending words: "The wanted child is the child that is planned; the child produced by the decision of the parent begins to look more and more like a technological product... A profound alteration in the relationship between parent and child may result when the child is no longer welcomed as a gift but produced as it were to order. Parental attitudes would thereby be affected, creating a sense of consumer ownership as well as a new anxiety to win and retain the child's affection."

Then he delivered the *coup de grâce*: "This attitude of parents conveys itself unconsciously to the child who experiences resentment against a parentage based on power and may result in the kind of teenage revolt we know so well."

And there it is. With a stroke he had insulted the estimated 90% or so of parents in the country who use contraception by saying that some of them might come to regard their children as products to place alongside their expensive car and collection of fine wines. Worse than that, he indirectly blamed teenage rebellion on parental use of contraception.

Given that talkback radio is turning the daytime audience of this country into candidates for the *Oprah Winfrey Show*, by expressing these sentiments Connell did the best impersonation of a suicide bomber I have ever seen in a long time. They were guaranteed to cause outrage and bring the roof crashing down on him.

By nature, Connell is an academic. A loyal son of the Church, he did not demur when he asked to become Archbishop of Dublin. Left to his own devices, however, he would probably have been happier to be left among his books at UCD. The age of the soundbite is not for him. He does not seem to realise the explosive impact a handful of words can have when condensed into a sensational headline and then thrown headlong into a society only waiting to be offended.

By overdrawing his argument, he distracted attention from the eminently defensible parts of his talk. For example, who can deny the condom and the pill are the best friends of a one-night stand? Before the arrival of effective contraception, the fear of pregnancy was too great to allow much in the way of extramarital and premarital sexual activity.

And who can deny that the promiscuity fuelled by the contraception has in turn fuelled the abortion rate? When contraception fails, or isn't used properly, then in many cases abortion will be resorted to as a back-up. Ireland's rising abortion rate bears ample testimony to this.

A very strong argument can be made in favour of contraception, one which the vast majority of people find convincing. Its widespread use has obviously changed society radically, but sometimes in ways that no reasonable person could defend.

What was striking about all those outraged commentators who filled the airwaves and the newspapers these past few days was that not one of them acknowledged that the so-called contraceptive culture is not all wine and roses. Who exactly is out of touch here?

Much worse, however, is the culture of political correctness that is suffocating people in Ireland. The sensitivity police are on constant patrol watching out for anyone who steps out of line, ready to bundle them into their Black Maria at the drop of a hat. Their latest bust is the Archbishop of Dublin. Someone is going to get promoted for this. These commissars of political correctness are successfully blackmailing into silence all those deemed insufficiently sensitive and caring. Perhaps in the end, though, we should stand back and admire these enlightened creatures if only for their finely tuned sense of proportion.

After all, who else but they would have spotted that Connell's 'insensitive' remarks were as outrageous as the allegations of corruption and cronyism pouring out of the tribunals very other day?

CHAPTER 6

CRISES FACING RELIGION AND POLITICS IS NO COINCIDENCE

2000

Today, without the aid of a safety net, I am going to attempt a truly death-defying feat. Flying in the face of received wisdom, I will try to demonstrate that not going to church every week is bad for you and bad for the nation.

And for my next trick, I will show the Irish government that the way to combat voter apathy is to combat religious apathy. For example, if you persuade more people to go to church each week, you will increase participation in the political process.

This is actually easier than it seems and hardly deserving of applause because the evidence that religious and political participation go hand-in-hand had been staring us in the face for a long time now.

The recent *Irish Times*/MRBI poll confirmed the fact. When I read the headline – Mass Very Important to Only 40% – the first thing that occurred to me was that four out of 10 was not bad. Given the buffeting the Catholic Church has received, it could easily have read: Mass Still Very Important to 40%.

I wondered whether the poll found that interest in politics was at the same level. Voting in general the election was seen as very important by 54%. Why didn't that sentence read "only" 54%, I asked myself. Since the finding about Mass contained that demoralising word, why not the finding about politics?

The poll also revealed, unsurprisingly, that the older the age group, the greater the degree of importance placed on Mass. Thus, almost three-quarters of respondents aged 65 or more said Mass was very important as against 14% of 18-24-year olds. What, I wondered, would have been found had the different age groups been asked about the importance of voting.

The next day, The *Irish Times* answered my question. This time the word 'only' turned up in the report, in the form of: "only one-quarter of the 18-24 age group regard it as 'very important' to vote in a general election." What's more, just as with the question about Mass, the older the respondent, the more likely it was that he or she would regard voting as very important, with 79% of pensioners seeing voting in this light.

The crisis facing religion is much the same as the one facing politics. They are crises of commitment, belief, and participation. They are a symptom of rising individualism, a failure on the part of religion and politics to answer the question, "what's in it for me?"

Due to the failure to answer it, voter turnout is dropping in tandem with church attendance. The drop in the number willing to stand for election, at whatever level, is more or less equivalent to the Catholic Church's vocations crisis.

In addition, the age profile of those turning up at political meetings is much the same as that attending church every Sunday – and the leadership of the main political parties is almost as old as the leadership of the churches. If the front bench of Fine Gael fell under a bus tomorrow, there is almost no rising generation within the party from which their replacements could be drawn. Labour is in much the same boat. Fianna Fáil is in only slightly better shape.

So strong is the coincidence between the decline of politics and the decline of religion that you can bet your bottom dollar if church attendance rises again, so will political participation. People who attend church seem to be, generally speaking, more civic-minded than those who do not, so if you get more people into church, you'll probably get them into politics as well.

The key lies in giving a satisfactory answer to the "what's in it for me?" question, which neatly brings me back to the second, harder part of my feat, namely demonstrating that church attendance is, generally speaking, good for you and the nation.

Since the question, 'what's in it for me?' is a practical, utilitarian one, I'll give a practical, utilitarian answer. I'll turn to the social sciences because there is a growing mass of evidence that church attendance or religious practice is indeed good for you.

Lots of studies testify to this. One entitled 'Why Religion Matters: The impact of religious practice on social stability', is a good place to look. It was produced by the Heritage Foundation in America, a conservative think-tank admittedly. But don't let that put you off, because this is a review of numerous studies rather than a study in itself. The studies it reviews were produced by institutions that run right across the ideological spectrum.

It turns out, for example, that those who practise a religion are less likely, on average, to suffer mental problems, including stress. This is contrary to popular perception. But too much emphasis has been placed on unhealthy religiosity and too little on the more common and healthier kind. These studies are finding that religious practise provides psychological protection.

They are also finding that churchgoers are more likely to be married, less likely to be divorced or single, and more likely to manifest high levels of satisfaction in marriage.

The regular practise of religion helps people move out of poverty. It generally inoculates individuals against a host of social problems including suicide, drug abuse, out-of-wedlock births and crime. There is a positive correlation between church attendance and physical health.

Most of these studies don't measure the depth of religious commitment. They generally go no deeper than asking a person if they go to church and pray regularly. Those who do measure the depth of religious commitment find the same positive correlations as above, only more so.

The reason the studies concentrate on regular church attendance is because it is the best indicator of religious practise. Religious practise in turn indicates a religious world-view, and it is this that explains why religion has beneficial effects on most practitioners. A religious world-view allows a person to place their worries and anxieties within a cosmic framework. This enables them to gain perspective. It allows them to step outside of themselves.

Religious practise sets up a sort of virtuous circle. By helping you to put meaning, shape and purpose to life, it gives you relative peace of mind, which helps you solve your personal problems, which has beneficial effects on your health, your family life, and even on work performance. This explains why religious practise, more than almost anything, provides a launching pad out of poverty. It leads to strong family life, and this breeds the confidence and self-esteem necessary for success in the outside world.

So it turns out that in response to the question, "What's in it for me?" we can answer, "plenty".

This means that the liberal left should think twice before celebrating the decline of religion. Few other things are better at combating poverty, tackling stress and mental health problems, keeping people off drugs and alcohol, cementing families, guarding physical health, and encouraging participation in politics and civil life.

The decline in church attendance is always presented as bad news for churches. In fact, it is much worse for societies.

CHAPTER 7

ABORTION DEBATE FALLS FOUL OF EMOTIONAL CARPET BOMBING

2001

Note: This article was written in the run-up to the abortion referendum of 2002

For years we have heard calls for a 'calm, reasoned' debate on abortion. Almost invariably, these calls have come from those who are either pro-choice, or at least from those who are opposed to a ban on abortion being enshrined in the Constitution.

The moral civil war that has raged over this issue has left many on the liberal side nursing deep wounds, even 10 and 20 years on, from the mauling inflicted on them by hysterical, emotional pro-lifers accusing them of being baby murderers and such like.

The issue remains unresolved. As a result of the X case decision of 1992, we must either legislate for that judgement or reverse it through another constitutional amendment. If it is not reversed, we pave the way for the enactment of a deeply-flawed decision, which, strictly speaking, allows abortion up until birth.

Bertie Ahern has unveiled a proposal that attempts to find a middle ground between the pro-choice position, and the pro-life position, as they exist in this country. That does not mean something halfway between Britain's regime of, effectively, abortion on demand, and our regime of no abortion at all. That would be politically and socially unacceptable in Ireland at present.

A halfway position in Irish terms is one that bans abortion, but permits the right to travel, the right to information, the morning after pill, as well as any treatment necessary to save the life of the mother, while taking account of the need to save the baby's life.

This was the government's attempt to reach a consensus on the issue that would avoid the bitterness of 1983 and 1992. That is still not a vain hope, although there are those on both sides who seem determined to make it so.

On the pro-life side, there are those who have convinced themselves that because the bill defines abortion as "the intentional destruction by any means of unborn life after implantation in the womb" it thereby withdraws protection from unborn life pre-implantation. Primarily because of this misinterpretation, some pro-lifers are on the point of rejecting the bill.

On the pro-choice side, agencies such as the Irish Family Planning Association simply want abortion on demand. The Labour Party wants the same, thanks to a policy outlined in a motion passed at its annual conference a few weeks ago.

Then there is Fine Gael. Fine Gael doesn't know what it wants, except it doesn't want this bill.

A considerable amount of bitterness and emotion is being generated by the pro-choice side, and this is the side that has consistently called for a 'calm, reasoned' debate.

Already some commentators have reached for the rhetorical equivalent of nuclear weapons. A cartoon in *The Sunday Tribune* compared pro-lifers to Islamic fundamentalists. Journalist Dick Walsh compared them to mullahs. The idea, of course, is that all religious fundamentalists are the same, according to which logic the impulse that leads one person to seek to protect life from the womb to the tomb is the same as that which leads another to fly a passenger plane into a skyscraper.

This sort of pro-choice rhetoric is the equivalent of the baby murderer accusations of the pro-life side. It is guaranteed to lead to a bitter and divisive referendum. Also guaranteed to do so is what we got from several Fine Gael deputies in the Dáil as the government bill reached the second reading stage.

Alan Dukes, the former Fine Gael leader, rounded on the government because its answers to the three dozen technical questions the party put to it about it were, well, technical. "The whole tone [of the answers] is mechanical, technocratic and dismissive of any hint of emotion." They don't show "compassion", he said. "A strong streak of misogyny runs through the responses."

Nora Owen, the Fine Gael deputy leader, also uttered the dread charge of misogyny. At the beginning of her 22-minute intervention in the debate, she described how she greeted news of the new bill with "anger", and how she was now angry again having heard some of the contributions in the house. So much for a 'calm' debate then.

She then rounded on the government for trying to remove the threat of suicide as grounds for permitting an abortion, and accused it of telling women that "their bodies are divided at the neck", meaning a woman can seek an abortion when her body requires it, but not when her mental condition does. This is tantamount, she said, to telling women that society wants to help them only when they are physically ill, not when they are mentally ill.

She expressed surprise that the psychiatric profession has not risen up in protest. Evidently, Owen paid little attention to the hearings to the Oireachtas sub-committee on abortion, where one psychiatrist after another said the threat of suicide is not reasonable grounds for an abortion.

She and Dukes also joined Senator Helen Keogh who, the previous day, had condemned the term "social abortion". What does this mean? Keogh had asked. Does it mean seeking an abortion between "painting their nails and having their hair done?"

What it means is an abortion carried out for means other than strictly medical ones. It means an abortion carried out on a woman who feels she simply cannot cope with a baby at this point in her life. The great majority of abortions fall into this category.

The essence of the argument being put by Owens, Dukes, Keogh and Monica Barnes, the Fine Gael TD, was that they have a monopoly on compassion, that only they truly know what women want, that only they have women's best interests at heart, and that anyone who opposes them, and supports this bill, must be a misogynist.

This tactic, far from opening up a debate, can only close it down. It amounts to an exercise in emotional carpet-bombing. It was moral blackmail of exactly the sort some pro-lifers have engaged in in the past. It was about as far removed from a 'calm, reasoned' debate as it could be.

There are, in the Fine Gael party, those who broadly support the government's approach. Gay Mitchell is one, John Bruton is another. Mitchell has fought hard to prevent his party rejecting this bill outright, but given the emotive approach of Dukes, Owen and company, it will probably be a losing battle.

This will leave Fine Gael with no coherent approach to abortion. It doesn't want this bill. It is not committed to X-case-style legislation. It is still far removed from adopting Labour's policy of seeking abortion on demand. So what does it want? This lack of a coherent position needs to be exposed.

CHAPTER 8

STUFF THE CULTURE, JUST TASTE
THAT RAMPANT CONSUMERISM

2002

The game is up. We've been busted. An article in the current issue of the *New Statesmen* exposes us as a bunch of poseurs more concerned with style than substance; as fools easily parted with our money.

The *New Statesman* has attacked one of Dublin's most fashionable eateries. After tearing to shreds Conrad Gallagher, the former star chef, it then has a go at the latest 'restaurant du jour', The Commons on St Stephen's Green in Dublin. The writer, Bee Wilson, claims: "This is bad food kept afloat by a giant bubble of hype and a city full of new cash. Sooner or later, as Conrad Gallagher discovered, the bubble will burst."

With our economy headed south, that may happen sooner rather than later, and that might be no bad thing if it punctures Dublin's insufferable sense of self-satisfaction.

Wilson writes that in Dublin today, it is easier to find pretentious Caesar salad than "honest Irish stew". She tells the tale of Gallagher, the boy from Donegal whose food was hyped beyond reason, who allowed his success to go to his head, who spent his money on a "Marco Pierre White hairdo, a £700,000 Dublin town house and some fancy paintings", and then lost everything.

She says that despite the fall of Gallagher, *haute cuisine* in Dublin carries on, and then she proceeds to skewer The Commons restaurant. The eatery has been described as "pricey but worth every penny". "Pricey is right," complains Wilson. "A dinner for two cost £120 (or €180). As for worth every penny? Well, yes, if you like... vinegary *lollo rosso*, manicured vegetables, logs of uncooked leeks, tasteless sauces, bland cheesecake and service that lectures you on the food before you are allowed to take a mouthful."

So, has an outsider discovered that the emperor has no clothes? Actually everybody in Dublin, nay everybody in Ireland, has tales of bad food and overpriced restaurants. Even a mid-priced restaurant will charge €100 for dinner for two and that's without downing too much wine.

So why do we put up with it? For two reasons: the first is relatively benign, the other is a terrible indictment of the way we live now.

The benign reason is that we have no choice: the whole country is overpriced. A pint in Dublin city centre costs more than the price of a halfway decent bottle of wine in France; a pub lunch as much as the main course in a restaurant in Spain.

But of course, in strict economic terms, there is no such thing as 'overpriced'. The market will bear whatever it will bear, no more and no less. If restaurants and pubs charge us an arm and a leg for sub-standard fare, it's because we're willing to hand over the arm and the leg. If we withheld our custom, prices would drop overnight. So why don't we?

Need you ask? If there weren't expensive restaurants and overpriced shops, how would we be able to show the world how much money we're making? What would be the point of all the longs hours, all the stress, all the battling through traffic, if we couldn't flash the cash on weekends?

The truth is that few people really go to Dublin's top restaurants for the food. Nobody hands over the price of a one-way ticket to New York for grub they can get for half the amount somewhere else. No, they go there for the status. Eating at posh restaurants is a way of saying to the world: "Look at me, I've arrived."

Dublin is fast becoming a cheap and anonymous imitation of a big English town. When Wilson said it was easier to get a Caesar salad than an honest Irish stew, she was making an important point - there is little that is authentically Irish about Dublin anymore.

It's odd. Every year the Irish middle-class heads off overseas for its annual holiday to the south of France or fashionable Tuscany. We go there for the sun, the food and wine, the scenery and the culture. We value these places for their authenticity. We like the fact that Tuscany is distinctively Italian, and that Languedoc is distinctively French. Then we come back home and avoid anything that is distinctively Irish. In other words, we like everyone else's culture but our own.

This is an especially middle-class failing. The middle class, generally speaking, prefers rugby and golf to Gaelic football and hurling.

Anybody's food is better than Irish food. (Actually, that's probably true.) Irish Catholicism is the worst religion ever, and Irish music is awful unless it comes in some flash, glitzy packaging such as Riverdance.

Why do we suffer from such an awful cultural cringe? I never thought I'd say it, but I think it's part of a post-colonial hangover. When people are colonised for long enough, they usually respond in one of two ways; either they react very strongly against the culture of the coloniser by over-embracing a semi-mythologised version of their own culture. Or else they begin to internalise the mentality of the coloniser. They begin to ape his ways, to seek his approval, and if that means having to turn against their own culture, then so be it.

The French and Italians haven't been colonised in centuries, and so their middle-classes are proud of their cultural achievements. In fact, one reason they have cultural achievements is precisely because it's been so long since they were colonised.

A few years ago I spent a weekend in the town of Eu in Normandy. Dublin's patron saint, Laurence O'Toole, died there more than 800 years ago while soliciting the favour of Henry II. Every year on the anniversary of O'Toole's death, hundreds of people of all ages from the town go on a little pilgrimage to the place where he is supposed to have died. The mayor sometimes takes part. The year I was there the mayor was a communist and he still took part.

Religious practice in Eu is low. More take part in the half-day pilgrimage than go to Mass in the town's churches each Sunday. They do so simply because it is a long-standing tradition of Eu and they are happy and proud to take part in it. They know such traditions give the town its character and personality.

In Dublin, we hardly know who Laurence O'Toole is, and no ceremony takes place to commemorate him. Even if one did, the great majority of us would avoid it like the plague because we're far too sophisticated to be seen dead at such a thing.

People who are embarrassed by their traditions, by their culture and by their religion are easy meat for consumerism. After all, what's left but piling up money and showing it off when everything else of value is scorned and mocked?

Fifty years ago *The Quiet Man*, starring John Wayne and Maureen O'Hara was made. It's the quintessential piece of paddywhackery, and while the Ireland it portrayed never really existed, many tourists continue to come here each year in search of it.

They can still find an echo of it in a few corners and pockets of the country, but increasingly we're the land found by Bee Wilson, a place full of people happy to hand over ludicrous amounts of money for "duck *confit* shredded in old rancid fat" as the price of looking good.

CHAPTER 9

FROM SAINT ANTHONY TO ELVIS, WE STILL REVERE RELICS

2003

Religion here is in steep decline and the churches soon will be half-empty. In a way, it's amazing they're not completely empty given the scandals, the lack of leadership in the Church, the growth of individualism, consumerism and all the rest of it.

But then along come the relics of Saint Anthony and tens of thousands of people turn out to see them. The same thing happened when the relics of Saint Therese arrived in Ireland two years ago.

This visit lasted only eight days, whereas the relics of Saint Therese toured the whole country. The Saint Anthony relics left Dublin just once — to go to Carlow, where about 50,000 people filed past them. Had they been able to stay in Ireland as long as the Saint Therese relics, you know that hundreds of thousands would have gone to see them as well.

To modern, secular-minded Ireland, the appeal of a saint's relics is a mystery. It is a superstitious throwback that could only interest the simple-minded and gullible.

Actually, their appeal has a very modern equivalent — the roaring trade in the relics of secular icons. Substitute the word "memorabilia" and consider the popularity of memorabilia connected with any famous person you care to mention. Think Marilyn Monroe, Elvis Presley or Princess Diana.

Monroe was the number one sex symbol of the 20th Century, probably the most recognisable woman of all time and still has tremendous resonance with millions of people. Is it so surprising that her most devoted fans would want items that belonged to her?

Cynics will say it makes perfect sense. Marilyn Monroe items have a resale value and that is why people buy them. Well, that might be the case sometimes but lots more people buy them without a thought of selling them on — simply because they like Marilyn Monroe.

If pop stars, films stars, sex symbols and royalty aren't your cup of tea, maybe it is a great political leader, writer or artist you have in mind. Perhaps you would prefer relics of John F. Kennedy. Or Mahatma Gandhi. Or James Joyce.

The Irish government paid a small fortune not so long ago to bring Francis Bacon's art studio to Dublin. To ensure that the studio was recreated exactly as it was in England, archeologists were hired to record where every item was placed and to put each back in that precise spot when the studio arrived in Dublin. If that is not an act of quasi-religious reverence, what is?

Almost everyone has someone or something that they revere or admire and, being physical creatures, we want a physical reminder of that person or thing. It's human nature. Why should it be any different for religious believers?

The sceptic will say that revering or admiring the memorabilia of a dead movie star or politician is not the same as venerating the relics of a saint. The sceptic will say the former is a rational act while the latter remains superstitious.

The person who collects an item that belonged to John F. Kennedy does not pray to him or look for favours from him, much less expect a cure. The religious believer who venerates a relic does so with one or all of these things in mind.

In fact, the religious believer is venerating not the relics but the saint to whom the relic once belonged. And the believer does not worship the saint as many people think. Nor does she (and it usually is a she) expect a favour or a cure from the saint, but rather through the saint.

There is little difference between asking your mother to say a few prayers so that you do well in your Leaving Cert and asking a saint to do the same. You are asking both your mother and your favourite saint to intercede with God on your behalf.

No doubt some people expect a cure or favour from the relic itself. And that is superstition. But that is not the theory and it usually isn't the practice either.

Furthermore, the religious believer who venerates a saint using a relic as an aid has something in mind beyond the relic itself. Ultimately, that something is God.

The person who collects Elvis Presley memorabilia has nothing in mind but Elvis Presley, or perhaps the investment value of his purchases. So which is more worthy, the fascination with secular relics or religious ones? There's not really so much room after all for the secular world to scoff at the religious because of their devotions to saints.

Nor is the veneration of saints peculiar to Catholicism. Almost all of the main religions, including Buddhism, Hinduism and Islam, have saints, relics and devotions.

What's ironic is that the same 'sophisticated' types who look down their noses on relics and grottoes, sacred statues and traditional devotions in Ireland think the opposite when they encounter them in India, Thailand or Bali.

In Thailand you will stumble across Buddhist shrines everywhere you go. Outside the temples you'll find traders selling every type of religious statue or image.

In the temples, monks often raise money by selling worshippers the Buddhist equivalent of the indulgences that so infuriated Martin Luther and led to the Reformation. In the Buddhist case, some temples promise a better reincarnation next time if you would only help them build a new temple or repair an old one.

But the self-same types who think these things are awful at home and want them put in the nearest basement, attic or dump think them a sign of a deep and rich culture overseas. And they're right, because almost anywhere you go in the world, culture is eight-tenths religion. Take away the religion and you don't have much left.

So why is the attitude so different when the 'sophisticates' are at home?

They are a bit like those who thought it was fine that the preamble to the forthcoming EU constitution mentioned the Greek and Roman part of European heritage and skipped over to the Enlightenment but ignored the thousand years of Christendom in between.

This is prejudice, pure and simple. And so is sneering at the veneration of saints. This veneration has its secular equivalent and if we think that's okay, we should think the religious version is too. And even if we don't, we should at least be prepared to lower the curled lip and put up with it.

Oddly, large parts of the Church don't much like relics either. Or at least they don't give much thought to them. They find them vaguely embarrassing.

Contrary to what a lot of people thought at the time, the visit of the relics of Saint Therese was not organised by the bishops. They gave it their approval, but the prime mover behind it was a Carmelite, Fr Linus Ryan. He never doubted that the visit would be a huge success and would confound all those who thought the veneration of saints could not possibly appeal in 21st-Century Ireland.

CHAPTER 10

FALSE CHILD ABUSE CLAIMS SHOW THE NEED FOR CAUTION

2003

Is it possible that people in Ireland could be falsely accused of child sex abuse? Absolutely.

A particularly horrendous example of this took place in Limerick recently. A teacher at a special school there was charged with sexually assaulting two mentally impaired youths. From the time the accusations were made until his acquittal last November, he lived as though under siege.

When the teacher was brought to Limerick district court to be formally charged, a crowd was waiting. The teacher and his solicitor, John Devane, were spat on, shouted at, pushed. Those who defended the teacher were vilified by members of the local community for siding with an 'abuser'. Colleagues feared they would be similarly accused. In the end more than 100 complaints of sexual abuse against children were made at the school. The two youths who accused the teacher made 48 allegations between them. Four related to the teacher himself.

During the trial, it transpired that gardaí investigating the case did not have the necessary qualifications for interviewing people with a mental handicap.

The teacher was acquitted following a unanimous verdict by the jury. After the trial John Devane declared: "The defence can't believe this case was brought to trial... I'm pointing the finger at the State authorities. This was a travesty of justice waiting to happen. It has ruined the last five years of the man's life and he will spend the next five years putting it back together again."

No matter what, some people will continue to suspect the teacher was guilty as charged. There is more than a whiff of the witch hunt about this, just as there was in the case of Nora Wall, the ex-nun accused of rape, sentenced to life in prison, only for the case against her to collapse.

First, there was the extreme readiness to believe the allegation, in contrast to our past refusal to accept such claims. The lawyer who defended the 'witch' or the alleged abuser was himself accused of a sex crime. Colleagues who came forward to defend the reputation of the accused teacher were effectively accused of being in league with 'witches'. A mob gathered at the court to attack the teacher — why put him on trial at all? This is dangerous stuff and it explains why those who work with children — men especially — now live in fear of being falsely accused of child abuse.

In the present atmosphere a man would have to think long and hard before becoming a priest or a teacher for example.

In response to these fears the head of the Council of Priests in Dublin, Fr Martin Cosgrove, has circulated a letter to his fellow clerics inviting a response about the matter.

He is concerned that the guidelines introduced by the bishops in the light of the sex abuse scandals are sometimes being implemented in such a way as to endanger a priest's right to his good name.

Arising from this concern, he writes, is "the possibility — indeed the reality — of false allegations and their consequences; the virtual impossibility of being able to have one's good name restored following such false allegations; the undermining of the presumption of innocence; the procedures involved when an accusation is made against a priest or religious (member of a religious order); and what procedures, if any, has the Church in place to vindicate the good name and reputation of a falsely accused priest or religious?"

The letter was prompted in particular by a current case involving a priest accused of child abuse who has stepped aside from his pastoral duties following a request from the Dublin diocese. Some senior priests feel the

because, by stepping down from his
priest's parishioners will suspect —
child abuse. Assuming he is cleared
recover his reputation?

ague is accused of child abuse, the
elines, but many would rather that
ge — be put under 24-hour supervi-
ties. In this way no children would
less danger of lasting harm being

a meeting on the strength of Fr
of the diocese and either Cardinal
bishop Diarmuid Martin.
gitimate because once an allegation
rd to restore the accused person's

al is done between Dublin's bishop
blic, it will look like the Church is
once again putting the wishes of its clerics ahead of the safety of children. In other words, it will find itself accused again of exactly the kind of clericalism that caused the Church to deal with these cases in the first place.

So if priests do want the implementation of the guidelines altered, then they must announce in public their intention of seeking such a change. They must argue the need for the change out in the open and not behind-closed-doors. If a meeting with the bishop does take place, the fact of the meeting must be made known and its outcome publicised and explained.

Only then can the charge of clericalism be avoided.

What the priests' concerns do highlight is that in any system of justice we need to balance the presumption of innocence against the need to apprehend and punish the guilty. When a subject is as heated as that of child abuse, it is very easy to lose the presumption of innocence. It seems that this is exactly what is happening.

CHAPTER 11

FOR HEAVEN'S SAKE, FEEL FREE TO EXPRESS YOUR BELIEFS

2003

The Pope has caused offence. Yet again. He has issued a 16,000-word document on the Eucharist. He devoted a few hundred words of it to reiterating the ban on Catholics receiving communion in Protestant churches. That caused the trouble.

This issue has a particular resonance in Ireland, partly because of President Mary McAleese's decision to defy the ban in 1997 when she was only a few weeks in office.

Cardinal Desmond Connell was prompted to make his by now infamous "sham" remark which many interpreted as a reference to Anglican communion — it had people waxing indignant over the airwaves for days afterwards.

Given that Ireland is becoming more secular by the hour, the Catholic teaching on inter-communion has an amazing ability to get us hot under the collar.

For some people, the reason is Northern Ireland. Obviously, the religious divide is a big contributor to tensions in the North. This being so, we think that anything which brings Catholics and Protestants closer together has got to be a good thing. And since inter-communion brings Catholics and Protestants closer together, who but a bigot or an obscurantist would prevent it, especially when lives might be at stake? A fair enough point, you might think, except it forgets that when Rome issues a ruling, it is with the entire Church in mind and not just isolated pockets of it. For Rome, the world does not start and end with Ireland.

Second, the argument exaggerates the ability of inter-communion to reduce inter-communal tensions. Two types of people are likely to present themselves for inter-communion. The first generally have a good opinion of their fellow Christians already and so are unlikely to want to discriminate against them for religious or any other reasons.

On the other hand, the sort of person who hates those who belong to other Churches is never going to present themselves for inter-communion. The second type doesn't really care for the theological differences between the Churches, in any case. They tend to be secular-minded, and so it's no skin off their noses to receive communion from whoever is offering it. They probably think it's all mumbo jumbo anyway and are almost certainly present in church for community or political reasons, as distinct from religious ones.

Since their motivation stems from politics, it's only politics, and not religion, that's going to bridge the gap that exists between two sides of the communal divide.

But the main thing annoying people about the Catholic ban on inter-communion — in the South at any rate — isn't its effect on Northern Ireland, rather it's that it seems so downright intolerant. Like Cardinal Connell, the Pope must think that Protestant communion is a sham, a cheap imitation of the real thing.

Except, of course, neither the Pope nor Cardinal Connell believes any such thing. When Cardinal Connell used the word "sham", he wasn't referring to Protestant communion at all.

What he was actually describing as a sham was the act of Catholics receiving communion from a Church with which their Church is not yet fully united. He meant that such an act implies full communion, when nothing of the sort exists. In that sense the act is a sham. If he was criticising anybody it was Catholics, and not Protestants, let alone what Protestants believe.

This goes to the heart of the matter. Protestants who allow inter-communion believe that shared communion will bring closer the day when full unity between the Churches is achieved.

Catholics, on the other hand, believe that shared communion is a sign of unity already achieved. It is what you do to signify that unity, and is not a step on the road to it.

In fact, without using the word sham, the Pope comes fairly close in his document on the Eucharist to echoing Cardinal Connell's statement when he gives one reason why the Catholic Church forbids inter-communion.

He writes: "The Catholic faithful, while respecting the religious conviction of their separated brethren, must refrain from receiving the communion distributed in their celebrations, so as not to condone an ambiguity about the nature of the Eucharist, and consequently, to fail in their duty to bear clear witness to the truth."

This is a matter close to home because I'm in a so-called 'mixed-marriage'. From time to time I attend my wife's church. Once a month, communion is celebrated in her church. I don't receive communion on such occasions because I think that to do so would send a signal that I am a member of her Church. If I ever do join it, then I will take communion with them. To do that now would be to put the cart before the horse as it were.

That said, between people who believe that shared communion is an aid to unity, and those who believe it can only be the sign of unity fully achieved, there is plenty of room for disagreement. This is an argument, in the main, between true believers.

However, there is another camp altogether whose profession of tolerance in this regard is actually barely disguised intolerance.

This camp believes their support for inter-communion is a sign of their open-mindedness, but it is really a sign of their contempt for sincerely held religious beliefs. In this camp are all those who think that the differences between the various religions are of no real consequence because religious beliefs are just man-made inventions to be discarded when they reach their sell-by date.

Between such people and religious believers like the Pope, there is an almost unbridgeable chasm. One reason the Pope wrote this latest encyclical was precisely to restate what Catholics believe the Eucharist to be. The last thing the Catholic Church believes is that the Eucharist is something man-made. It believes that it is God-given and therefore treats it with the utmost seriousness. It is not something that can be compromised away in order to satisfy a constituency that doesn't believe anything is God-given.

In fact, there is now a growing number of people who are offended by the very act of somebody professing a religious belief. If a Christian says that Jesus is "the way, the truth, and the life", we are told that Hindus, Buddhists, Muslims etc. will be offended. If the Catholic Church says it is the one true Church, we are told that Protestants will be offended. In order to avoid giving offence, religious believers are increasingly being told to keep their beliefs to themselves.

This, they are told, is what it means to live in a tolerant, pluralist, liberal society.

But surely tolerance is about allowing people to express beliefs we don't like, and surely the very essence of intolerance is forbidding people from saying what they believe? If the Catholic Church believes it is the one true Church, then it is entitled both to hold and state that belief. What it is not allowed to do is impose it on others.

And if it believes that the Eucharist is so important that it cannot be shared until full unity between the Churches is achieved, it must be permitted both to hold that belief and express it. It is one thing to disagree with it. It is quite another to try to suppress it entirely in the name of a bogus tolerance.

CHAPTER 12

ON LOSING MY MOTHER

2003

When you are waiting for a loved one to die, time takes on a different quality. The outside world seems to disappear into the distance, a shimmer on the horizon as you enter another world, one suspended between life and death.

This was the experience of my family last month. My mother, Alice Quinn, aged 70, had been struck down by a stroke on the Saturday and died on the following Thursday morning, just as dawn was breaking. Three of us were present when it happened. The words 'she breathed her last' are just a literary flourish until you actually witness someone breathing their last.

Each breath becomes shallower, the gaps between each one become longer as you sit beside the bed wondering when the final breath will come. And then it comes, and having accompanied your loved one to death's door you can go no further and you draw back and try to re-enter the world of the living.

That's not easy at first. The philosopher Dietrich von Hildebrand probably spoke for countless people in the same situation when she said: "I am filled with disgust and emptiness over the rhythm of everyday life that goes relentlessly on — as though nothing has changed, as though I have not lost my precious beloved."

There is something to be said for the old custom of wearing a black armband when a family member dies. It tells the outside world of your bereavement and you are given a certain amount of space for a while.

The Victorians overdid the mourning. Queen Victoria mourned her husband Albert until her own death 40 years after his. That was excessive, even by the standards of the day, but we probably underdo it. It's as though we don't know how to relate to death, or even that we don't want to relate to it even though we all must eventually.

Most people probably reach middle-age before they lose anyone truly close to them. Only the unlucky ones lose a loved one before that.

Certainly nobody close to me had died before my mother, and I don't think you can fully appreciate just how great a loss the death of a loved one can be until it happens to you. The experience of loss is probably the greater when the death is unexpected — as it was in my mother's case — and when the person who has died is still relatively young.

Alice Quinn was an active 70-year-old. Her own mother had died only nine years before. Sixty-one is a more fitting age at which to see off a parent. Anything else seems too early.

My mother was part of a generation of women that is now, literally, dying off. She was formed in an Ireland that is dying off with it. It was a generation that was born into an Ireland that had only recently gained independence and was unsure of itself politically, but was sure of itself morally. Its values were those suited to a rural society and were grounded in the certainties of the Catholic Church. It was also a generation that saw those values and certainties swept away.

Previous generations of Irish people were forced to live through great political and economic upheavals, but my mother's generation witnessed a revolution in values such as had not been seen in centuries. My generation lives on the other side of that revolution. We didn't have to make any dramatic adjustments to our thinking. We can take the revolution, both the good and bad aspects of it, for granted. My parents' generation was either carried along by it helplessly, resisted it bitterly, or in some cases applauded it and helped it along.

The revolution affected women in particular. My mother was born in 1932, but had she been born in 1962 how might her life have turned out? She was lucky enough to receive a secondary education, following which she worked as a clerk for a few years. After that she got married, and as was the custom, and in many cases the requirement, she gave up paid employment forever.

Had she been born a couple of decades later she would have been young enough to benefit from some of the gains of feminism. She would have been more likely to go on to third-level education and maybe then into a career at which she might have worked until retirement.

Or would it have made that much of a difference to her life? After all, even today most women (and a lot of men) don't have careers, and many don't even want one. I suspect my mother would have fallen into this category, even if she had been born later.

If she had remained in the workplace after having children, she would have done so not for the love of it, but because of the modern tyranny of the two-income mortgage. While the women of that generation had to give up work, like it or not, once they got married or after the first child arrived, many women stay on in work now because of the price of houses. Being pre-feminist, my mother didn't think of it in terms of rights. She didn't know how to. Thanks to feminism, we now know that this can be a disaster for women. A bullying husband can take advantage of such a woman's inbred impulse always to put others before herself. My mother was lucky enough not to be married to such a person.

But if not thinking in terms of your rights can be bad for a marriage, so can thinking too much in terms of them. There's a very short distance between an over-emphasis on personal right and self-fulfilment and the divorce courts.

My mother spent the last days of her life surrounded at various times by her husband, her four children, 11 grandchildren, and some of her relatives from her native Limerick.

In the future such a scene will be less common than it is today. A lot of people are going to die lonely deaths. Our increasing divorce rate means a growing number of people are going to die with no spouse to hand. Divorced men might also die estranged from their children.

We have fewer children than our parents. There's nothing wrong per se with small families, but larger ones are usually better able to act as support networks.

Women of my mother's generation made a career of their families and usually succeeded in bringing up a great store of human as distinct from material wealth. This often required tremendous personal sacrifice, but then anything worthwhile does.

Old Ireland is held in considerable contempt today. We think it was small-minded, repressive, joyless, insular, ignorant and uneducated. But all of us grew up with the products of that Ireland; our parents.

While plenty of us probably had parents who fitted perfectly into the most negative stereotype of old Ireland, many more did not. We don't remember our mothers and fathers as small-minded or ignorant, or as repressed and joyless. We remember them as people who put our needs before their own.

And they were like this not in spite of the sort of Ireland in which they were raised, but because of it. That was an Ireland which thought in terms of the needs of family and community first, and the individual second. Sometimes a high price was paid for this because sometimes individual rights must be asserted. But if that Ireland was as bad as is commonly painted, why do we so often admire and love so much the people it produced?

CHAPTER 13

THE POPE'S FUNERAL WAS A SYMBOL OF THE UNIFYING POWER OF RELIGION

2005

The whole world beat a path to the funeral of Pope John Paul II last week. That's a curious thing, don't you think? By now the papacy was supposed to be a faded force in history and yet more world leaders attended the funeral on Friday than attended the funeral of any other person, ever.

About 200 world leaders were at the funeral of Pope Paul VI in 1978. Twice that number attended the funeral of Pope John Paul. But that only tells half the story, because it wasn't only the number that went up, it was also the level of seniority.

In 1978, the then US President Jimmy Carter, sent his wife. This time the President himself came. And so did the other President Bush, and so did Bill Clinton. US Secretary of State Condoleezza Rice was there too.

In all, 2,500 representatives of the governments of the world were in St Peter's Square last Friday. The leaders were each allowed to bring selected guests as well.

For me, the most noteworthy aspect of this cast of world leaders was the presence of so many Muslims. The King and Queen of Jordan were there. So was the President of Syria, and so was the President of Iran, who is also a Muslim cleric.

How could this be? Isn't religion supposed to be a divisive force in the world? And aren't Christianity and Islam the two faiths that are supposed

to be most at loggerheads? And yet here was the President of arguably the most militantly Islamic nation in the world attending the funeral of a Pope. It's a long way from the Crusades. And it's a long way from Muslim invasions of Europe.

Last Friday was a day that showed the unifying power of religion. When it came to the moment in the Mass when the congregation exchanged the Sign of Peace, the world leaders did exactly that. President Mary McAleese witnessed the Presidents of Israel and Syria shaking hands warmly despite the fact that their countries are bitter enemies and are still technically at war.

The President of Israel also shook hands with the President of Iran. Amazingly, the two men were born in the same town and, now, this Jew and this Muslim were meeting for the first time at the funeral of a Christian leader.

During his Pontificate the Pope's critics often accused him of being a divisive force. Well, this was well and truly given the lie by the reaction to his death and to his life. Paradoxically, this most important of Catholic Popes, one who, in a quite uncompromising manner, asserted the central beliefs of his Church, became a figure of unity.

This also gives the lie to the notion that the only way you can rebuild relations with those who differ from you is by compromising your own beliefs. The Pope did not do this and the result is that he appeared authentic to others, a true representative of his faith. People knew where they stood with him.

And from where he stood, confident in himself, confident in his beliefs, but never arrogant or triumphalist, he reached out the hand of friendship and many took it. They knew he was the head of the Catholic Church, but they also knew he was a man of peace and a man of God. It was on this level that Muslims, and those of other faiths, could relate to him. It is for this reason they attended his funeral.

As Pope, John Paul II was the leader of the Catholic Church. As a man of God and a man of peace, he was a world leader, in fact the pre-eminent world leader of the last 25 years. The Church won't see his like again for 500 years.

Sometimes a life is so well lived that when it is finished all we can do is stand back and applaud. Our reaction to the Pope's life was like the reaction of an audience to a classical masterpiece played for the first time, and to perfection, by a first-class orchestra led by a world-renowned conductor. When the piece is over, when the last note is played, when the conductor has put down his baton, so moved have we been by it, that we spontaneously, in one moment, rise to our feet, applaud loudly and shout: "*Bravisimo! Bravisimo!*" That is how the world reacted when the last and poignant note of Karol Wojtyla's life was played out before a massive worldwide audience at 9:37pm on Saturday, April 2, 2005. There was no other way to react, and the beauty of it was in the spontaneity.

Here's another curious aspect of this last fortnight. Hundreds of millions of people clearly admired this man, but many in his own Church did not. His conservatism frustrated the liberals, and the ire of the liberals caused the faint-hearted to, well, faint away. The faint-hearted included quite a few clergy. This meant we had the rather odd sight last week of clerics at various levels of seniority, who, with few exceptions, had never before spoken out so loudly in favour of the late Pope, suddenly doing so. And why? Because suddenly it was the popular thing to do. Where were they when it wasn't popular? They were nowhere to be seen.

When the sort of Catholicism favoured by the Pope comes under fierce and sustained critical scrutiny again, where will they be? Again in hiding.

CHAPTER 14

ALL COUPLES SHOULD BE GIVEN CERTAIN RIGHTS AND PROTECTIONS

2007

*Note: This column was written as a law to permit
same-sex civil partnership was underway.*

If gays and lesbians are to be given the same rights as married couples, then why not other couples as well? This is the question the Labour party must answer. So must all others who want to create gay marriage or its functional equivalent.

The question is especially urgent for Labour because this week it reintroduced into the Dáil the gay civil partnerships Bill it first put before the House last February.

For those who support the rights of gays and lesbians to marry, or enter civil partnerships that are marriage in all but name, the issue is very straightforward. It is all about non-discrimination and treating people equally.

But the Labour party needs to seriously consider the case of the Burden sisters which is currently before the European Court of Human Rights. If it doesn't, it will have no credibility whatever on this issue.

Joyce and Sybil Burden live in England. They are in their 80s and have lived together as spinsters for all of their lives. When one dies, the survivor is going to have to sell the home they have shared for decades because the remaining sister won't be able to pay the inheritance tax.

The Burdens wonder why a lesbian couple in a similar circumstance won't have to do this. It's an excellent point. Like the lesbian couple, the Burdens are a couple. Like the lesbian couple, the Burdens are both women. Like the lesbian couple, the Burdens are in a loving, committed relationship.

What's the difference, therefore? What's the justification for imposing inheritance tax on one loving committed relationship and not the other? The only real difference between the Burdens and the lesbian couple is that the relationship between the Burdens is not sexual and the relationship between the lesbian couple is. This is the one and only thing that really separates the two couples and the British government obviously thinks that sex is so vastly important that one of the Burdens will have to sell their long-time family home when the other dies and the lesbian couple won't.

The Irish Labour party, if it was clever enough, might concede that the only real difference between the Burdens and the lesbian couple is indeed that one relationship is sexual and the other isn't. But it could then point out that this is also the only real difference between the Burdens and a married couple.

In pointing this out, they would be forcing people who are pro-traditional marriage, rather than themselves, to explain what is so important about sex, that sexual relationships get all sorts of public benefits that other forms of relationships don't get.

Very well then, let's answer it. Let's make it as clear as possible. The reason married couples receive certain benefits from society has nothing to do with sex *per se*. The liberals are right, neither the State nor society has any compelling interest in the sexual relationships of its citizens, assuming those relationships are consensual and not harming anyone.

It's not the fact that a married couple is having sex that interests the State. It's what the sex generally produces that interests the State, namely children. This is what separates a married couple from a gay or lesbian couple, or from the Burdens. The gay couple, the lesbian couple and the Burden sisters cannot have children together unless they adopt or avail of IVF and neither of these things involves sexual intercourse. (Incidentally, if we think two lesbians should be able to adopt or use IVF, then why not two sisters or two brothers?)

Labour and all other advocates of same-sex marriage/civil unions have completely lost sight of the fact that marriage is not really about recognising an adult relationship at all. As a social institution, it is primarily about children.

The reason a married couple is exempted from inheritance tax has to do with children. The reason they can share their tax allowances has to do with children. The reason one can inherit the pension of the other has to do with children. These benefits exist so that one or other spouse, usually the wife in practise, can give up work for some part of her career to stay at home and raise the children and not have to worry unduly about her pension or what will happen to the house when her husband dies.

Take children out of the equation and there is little public justification for attaching the benefits of marriage to anyone at all. There is, mind you, a justification for giving some of the benefits of marriage to couples, whether in conjugal relationships or not, but there is no justification for creating the functional equivalent of marriage for anyone other than married, heterosexual couples.

Labour thinks the issue is equality. It's not. The issue is children and the fact that marriage is publicly supported not for the sake of the adults, but because it is the most pro-child of social institutions. Unfortunately, this central public purpose of marriage has been obscured by a thick fog of 'rights talk' and dim-witted political correctness.

CHAPTER 15

LIBERALS ARE OBSTRUCTING ROAD TO CHRISTIAN UNITY

2007

*Note: In 2007, the Vatican published a document deal-
ing with areas of disagreement with other Churches that
sparked a row over ecumenism.*

The Gaelic Athletic Association bestrides its world like a colossus. Since its foundation over a century ago it has completely dominated hurling and Gaelic football.

I haven't got the foggiest notion about the internal politics of the GAA
and know even less about how GAA followers feel about the way the association runs its two codes.

But let's suppose for the sake of the argument that someday a sizable
number of football and hurling fans decided that they weren't happy with
the way the GAA was running things and decided to set up their own rival
organisation calling it, say, the Gaelic Athletic Society, or GAS for short.

Let's go even further and suppose that GAS was powerful enough to
actually seize some football grounds from the GAA and had the temerity to
claim that it and not the GAA was the true representative of the traditions
of hurling and Gaelic football in this country.

Now, how do you imagine the GAA would react to this?

One has to think it would react in much the same way the Catholic
Church reacted when Protestantism appeared on the scene almost 500 years
ago and challenged its authority.

It would fight back (hopefully not violently) and at the very least it would
assert that the newcomer was an upstart and that it, namely the GAA, was
the one true representative of hurling and Gaelic football.

Last week the Vatican issued a document asserting once again its claim that it is the one Church founded by Christ and calling into question the credentials of other Churches, especially the Protestant Churches which it calls 'ecclesial communities'. As is always the case whenever the Catholic Church has the nerve to reiterate an old and exclusive claim like this, there were howls of protest. Such a claim, we were told, is offensive and completely inappropriate when Christian unity should be at the top of every Church's agenda.

But in many spheres of life contests rage over who or what is the true representative of this or that idea, person or tradition. They go on in sport where, to name but one split, there are numerous boxing associations all offering rival boxing titles. They also go on in politics, sometimes to violent effect. The left has been bedevilled by rival claims over who is the true representative of, for example, the working class or the trade union movement. They go on between rival nationalist groups all the time. Just check out the history of this country.

If these rivalries go on in so many secular spheres, why is it so surprising that they go on in religion as well?

With respect to its claim to be the truest representative of Christianity on earth the Catholic Church presents us with a very simple question; did Jesus Christ found a Church or not and if so, which one?

Not without justification, the Catholic Church points out that it is the only universal Church which can trace itself all the way back to Christ and the Apostles, and then all the way to the present again through the successors of the Apostles, namely the bishops.

At the very least this is a defensible claim and in fact the existence of the bishops, gathered around the Pope, is the best and only guarantee of true Christian unity there is.

As we know, Protestantism is prone to endless divisions because there is no central authority that can adjudicate disputes over rival interpretations of the Bible. In the absence of such a body, not only is final unity impossible, the splits can, and will, only get worse.

The liberal solution to the divisions within Christianity is to dilute the core doctrines of Christianity and make them all optional extras, except perhaps for belief in Christ.

This sounds very neat, except that everyone has core beliefs they don't want to compromise away, and that includes liberals.

Right now, the biggest blows against Christian unity are being struck not by alleged doctrinal hardliners like Pope Benedict, but by liberals.

In the name of gay rights, for example, liberals are destroying the unity of the Anglican Communion and are driving a wedge between it and both the Catholic Church and the Eastern Orthodox Churches. But they think the price is worth it because, for them, gay rights are non-negotiable. In this respect they believe, nay they know, that they have the truth, the One Truth.

Liberals who object to the Catholic Church asserting it is the One, True Church don't really believe that there is no such thing as the Truth, as their uncompromising adherence to all kinds of principles, including gay rights, attests.

What they really believe is that they have the Truth and the Catholic Church doesn't, or to put it another way, they believe they are the One True Church. The reason they are angry at the Catholic Church is that it won't surrender to it.

What they want, in effect, is a take-over and documents such as the one the Vatican released last week delay what they hope is their inevitable triumph.

CHAPTER 16

DARK NIGHTS OF THE SOUL
IN MOTHER TERESA'S LIFE

2007

News that Mother Teresa suffered a 40-year-long crisis of faith during which she sometimes doubted even the existence of God will bring much comfort to atheists. Not that they need much, what with the slew of bestsellers on our shelves reassuring them that God really doesn't exist.

Stories of how people came to lose their faith or doubt their faith are much more popular these days than stories of how people came to believe in God, or else were constantly nagged by the suspicion that maybe, after all, he exists.

But such stories are plentiful and include some very prominent atheists and agnostics.

One was the famous English journalist and writer, Malcolm Muggeridge. Coincidentally, it was he who made Mother Teresa famous with his 1969 documentary, *Something Beautiful for God.*

There was GK Chesterton, who went on to become one of the greatest ever Catholic apologists. But some of the biggest-hitting atheists of the last few decades, intellectual heavyweights several classes above a Richard Dawkins or Christopher Hitchens, among them AJ Ayer and Anthony Flew, came in later life to doubt aspects of their non-belief.

Just a few years ago Flew came to the conclusion that there may be a Creator after all because the universe is so massively improbable, although he still does not believe in the Christian God. AJ Ayer never came to any sort of belief in God, but after a very unpleasant, hell-like near-death experience, he wrote that his disbelief in an afterlife had "weakened somewhat".

For some atheists these revelations were as shocking as the revelation that Mother Teresa generally experienced only "silence and emptiness" when she prayed. We never like to think that our heroes, upon whom our world view partly depends, doubted some of the things we counted on them to believe with fervour. That goes for everyone, atheists and religious-believers alike. It happens in politics too. Imagine the reaction if Bertie Ahern suddenly quit Fianna Fáil, joined the Labour party and ran for the leadership.

In fact, this is not the first time we've heard that Mother Teresa complained of having an arid spiritual life. It was also covered four years ago. What has put it back in the news is the publication of a book called *Mother Teresa: Come Be My Light,* containing 40 of her letters and edited by Fr Brian Kolodiejchuk, a close friend.

The letters are often anguished and angst-ridden, revealing a life of considerable pain behind the smiling public face. How this would have been grist to the mill of the late existentialist director, Ingmar Bergman whose most famous films dealt with doubt.

At one point Mother Teresa writes: "I am told God loves me, and yet the reality of the darkness and coldness and emptiness is so great that nothing touches my soul. I have no faith. I dare not utter the words and thoughts that crowd in my heart." Bergman could not have scripted better.

What these letters explode is the myth that she was a woman of simple faith. Her faith was anything but simple, much less simple-minded. Her letters are the product of a woman who thought deeply and intelligently about belief and unbelief, meaning and meaninglessness.

For a religious believer the letters of Mother Teresa might seem discomforting. We might like to think that a Mother Teresa, of all people, would feel God in her life as an active presence every day and that her prayers would always be responded to in an unmistakable way and that she experienced a daily mystical union with God. We might think that if she didn't experience such a thing, then who would?

On the other hand, the spiritual lives of the saints are as varied as the saints themselves, and while many saintly people have experienced 'dark nights of the soul' like Mother Teresa, others have felt, and feel, the presence of God each day.

In any event, no matter what Mother Teresa experienced through prayer, it would not make the least bit of difference to an atheist who would put any experience down to her imagination playing tricks on her. Let's remember that atheists like Richard Dawkins think that even love is simply a chemical reaction in our brain. If they can reduce love to that, they can certainly do the same to a religious experience.

Should we think more or less of Mother Teresa now that we know what we know about her inner spiritual life? Probably more. Her essential goodness is not in the least diminished by these letters. She still lived a life utterly devoted to God and to the service of others and while her prayer life wasn't what she hoped it would be, she persevered regardless.

In fact, these letters should recommend her to an age that celebrates religious doubt, and actively encourages it. She is, and will remain, a saint to Catholics. But her inner doubts should now endear her more to an age plagued by doubt. If she can doubt, but still believe, it gives believers permission to have doubts, and doubters permission to have beliefs.

CHAPTER 17

FATHER, FORGIVE THEM,
FOR THEY KNOW NOT…

2007

It is a pretty neat trick to get through 14 years of school and come out the other end without knowing what Easter is about or that Bethlehem is the reputed birth place of Jesus.

It's only a small exaggeration to say that it's a bit like going through life without ever knowing that Dublin is the capital city of Ireland. Some things should be part of general knowledge, including a rudimentary knowledge of religion.

But an opinion poll released earlier this week has found that levels of religious knowledge are shockingly low, especially among the 15-24 age group, that is the age group either still in school or not long out of school, which is to say the age group most recently exposed to religious education. Surely they should be the best informed?

The same poll revealed that it is the over-65s who have the most knowledge of religion, that it is those longest out of school. How does it come about that the older you are the more you know about religion, and the closer you are to school the less you know?

In a way, the answer is in the question; older people are more interested in religion, and younger people a lot less so.

Older people 'got' religion from the home, from school, from the parish, from the surrounding culture. It was hard not to 'get' religion. In say,

1950, it would have taken a special kind of genius to get through life without knowing what the Church celebrates at Easter.

This whole system of acquiring religious knowledge is now in a state of collapse. If the parents aren't interested in religion then they're not going to be passing it on to their children, and if they aren't interested in religion then they're not going to be attending the local church either. That's two of the means of knowledge transmission gone. This has a knock-on effect. The fewer people there are who have rudimentary religious knowledge, the less that knowledge will be part of general knowledge, meaning people won't acquire it from the surrounding culture either.

That leaves schools. What's going on there? Herein lies a tale, and a rather sad and sorry one. One big reason why older people can rattle off answers to questions like, 'what's the first commandment' is because they learned it by rote, through endless memorisation. The thinking was that even if a child did not understand the answers they were learning, at least they would have learned it and the understanding could come later.

But some time around 1970 there was the enormous rebellion against this kind of learning across the educational system generally and nowhere was the rebellion more successful, or more radical, than in the area of religious education. The new thinking said that rote learning was too mechanical, allowed no room for the pupil creativity and was deeply alienating to boot. It turned pupils off religion.

In addition, the old method approached religion in wholly the wrong way. Religion isn't primarily about knowledge, the new thinking went. It's about experience. It isn't so much about where knowing Jesus was born or even that he died and rose again, but about following Jesus' example. But it had, and has, a huge drawback.

Firstly, it's badly done. It's all colouring books and silly stories. But it threw out too much of the knowledge component as well. It doesn't ensure that pupils leave the school system having acquired the basics of faith.

Knowing where Jesus was born and what is celebrated at Easter is kindergarten stuff. It's something a child only halfway through primary school should know. It's an educational scandal when a 15-year-old doesn't know it. And it is no excuse to say that many parents are not passing on this kind of knowledge to their children either. A lot of parents don't bother to help their kids with reading or maths, but that would be no excuse if kids left school without being able to read or do basic sums.

It's obviously simplistic to blame the current lamentable state of religious knowledge on schools alone, or even schools primarily. There are many excellent teachers doing their best and they are up against it when the parents couldn't care less.

But what this poll should achieve, if it achieves nothing else, is to send a loud and clear message to those parents who do care. The message is that, with respect to religious education, it is only safe to assume your children know nothing and then take appropriate remedial action. You might discover they know quite a lot, but then again, you might discover they don't know a thing. There's only one way to find out: ask them.

CHAPTER 18

SEGREGATION CLAIM A SLUR AGAINST CATHOLIC SCHOOLS

2008

Critics have been pummelling Catholic primary schools these last few months, accusing them variously of being 'divisive', of causing 'segregation', even of fostering 'educational apartheid'. Now it transpires that these self-same schools are owed an exceedingly large apology.

The accusation that Catholic schools are divisive gained traction last September when we discovered that an emergency school had to be established in Balbriggan in north county Dublin for children from African backgrounds. Most of the media coverage verged on the hysterical. It was a case of 'Balbriggan Burning'. Next up, a movie of the same name with the Catholic Church standing in for the Ku Klux Klan.

It then turned out that the mess in Balbriggan wasn't the result of 'educational apartheid' at all, but rather of bad planning. If the local authorities had expanded the existing schools, the immigrant children could have been accommodated without a problem. But we didn't hear too much about that and so the image of the Deep South circa 1961 stuck in people's minds.

At the time, Catholic education bodies tried to point out that their schools accommodate plenty of non-national children. But they weren't listened to. It didn't suit certain agendas which are intent on bringing an end to denominational education.

But now we know that Catholic primary schools are accommodating more than their fair share of immigrant children, and Traveller children, and children with 'special education needs'. We know this because the Department of Education has carried out an audit of both primary and secondary schools aimed at discovering how many children from the above categories are present in their student populations. The audit can be found on the Department of Education website and received much (hysterical) coverage this week.

Catholic primary schools, like other denominational schools, do give preference to children of their own faith. This is why they exist. This is why many parents want them. But they are blind to a child's social background, or educational standard.

The fact that the audit effectively exonerates Catholic schools has been almost completely ignored. But Catholic education officials shouldn't ignore it. They should quote the audit every time Catholic schools are faced with the appalling charge of being segregationist.

The coverage of the report, having virtually ignored what the audit reveals about Catholic schools, instead highlighted what the report supposedly reveals about secondary schools, and what it supposedly reveals is that it is secondary schools that are fostering, you guessed it, educational apartheid.

The audit has found that some secondary schools have far more children from non-national and Traveller backgrounds, or with special education needs, than others. But is this evidence of 'apartheid'? It would be if certain schools explicitly barred children simply because they were immigrants or because they were Travellers. But that would be illegal and no school has such an enrolment policy.

What some schools do have is a policy that favours family members of past and present pupils over others. Maybe this should be reviewed, but with an open mind that doesn't automatically dismiss it as an option.

However, what is generally happening across the country, and what in most cases explains the clustering of certain children in certain schools, is that children from a given social background generally live in the same areas and go to the same schools.

To borrow a cliché, this is not rocket science. If you go to a school in a middle-class area you will find in that school mostly middle-class children. You probably won't find any Traveller children because Travellers don't tend to live in middle-class areas. Nor will you find many immigrants because immigrants usually can't afford to live in middle class areas.

Nor, for that matter, will you find many children with 'special educational needs' for the simple reason that middle-class parents invest so much time and energy in the education of their children. The result is that in national tests of reading and maths, their children tend to score well. This means they generally don't qualify as having 'special education needs'.

Unless you favour bussing children from middle-class areas to working-class areas, and vice versa in order to mix the social classes, there is absolutely no solution to this. But to bus children back and forth in this way would be social engineering on a grand and completely unacceptable scale. It would also be vastly unpopular with many parents. In fact, such a move would be deeply undemocratic and involve such a degree of State interference in our lives as to be virtually totalitarian.

This is the nub of the issue. Once you convince yourself that the present composition of our schools is the result of 'educational apartheid', the only real solution is State interference of almost Stalinist dimensions. The 'cure' is far worse than the alleged disease. And let's be clear, the disease is a myth. It's true that different social groups are to be found in different schools. But this isn't 'apartheid'. It's simply the way societies naturally organise themselves.

CHAPTER 19

DADDY MUST GO, HE'S NOT POLITICALLY CORRECT

2008

Trying to work out and reconcile the convoluted logic of political correctness is a full-time job. A gay man donates sperm to a lesbian couple and then tries to increase his access to his child against the couple's wishes. Who is a liberal to side with? The lesbians as it turns out. The man may be gay but he's still a man and that counts against him.

Or who to side with in the dispute over whether or not Muslims schoolgirls should be allowed to wear headscarves? Headscarves in Western eyes are a symbol of female oppression but on the other hand, Muslims are a minority group, long oppressed by us Westerners. This is a tough call which is why liberals appear to be divided on this one.

Or what about a child's need for a father? A few months ago, the women's studies unit at the University of Uppsala in Sweden produced a report that highlighted the importance of fathers in the development of children. Just last week, to coincide with International Day for Families, the UN produced a document that also highlighted the importance of fathers.

Why would impeccably PC bodies such as a women's studies unit or the UN produce reports showing the need for fathers who are men, after all, and therefore oppressors? The answer is that they have suddenly cottoned on to the fact that full female equality (as they define it) can't be achieved until fathers spend much more time with their children, thus freeing up women to spend more time in the workplace. These reports are therefore being used to justify more paternity leave and so on.

But try to use these same reports to justify say, marriage, and it's a whole other story. If you want fathers to have as much involvement with their children as possible, it makes sense to support marriage. In general, married men spend more time with their children than separated fathers or single fathers. But this won't do because supporting marriage might mean giving less support, relatively speaking, to other family forms and that would be 'judgemental' and 'discriminatory'.

Or if children benefit from having a father, as the University of Uppsala and the UN insist they do, based on lots of evidence, then surely lesbian parenting can't be such a good idea since by definition the father gets left out or has a part-time role at best?

But that won't do either because lesbians are a minority group and even though liberals are willing to support more paternal involvement in the lives of children, if that advances the goal of female equality, they won't support it if it means denying lesbian couples their 'right' to a child. Therefore, we have the absurdity of PC organisations saying on the one hand that fathers are needed, only to turn around when it suits them and say they're not needed.

The House of Commons decided on Tuesday night that fathers are not needed. It decided this in the context of a debate on a new Human Fertilisation and Embryology Bill. Up until now, fertility clinics in the UK were forced by law to at least pay lip-service to a child's need for a father. But no more. That requirement has been abolished. In one fell swoop, one of the most influential parliaments in the world decided children don't need fathers. Today Britain, tomorrow Ireland?

It really is astounding what is happening and how swiftly it is happening. In order to show a kind of tolerance – a deeply irrational kind – to a very small but very powerful and vociferous minority group, we are willing to declare that children don't need fathers and don't have a right to fathers.

In our state of deep self-delusion, we have convinced ourselves that recognising the right of single women or lesbian couples to avail of fertility services has no consequences beyond the happiness of the adults involved.

What we have forgotten is that a child has a right to a father and a father has a right to his child.

But when we are reminded of these rights, as happened in Britain this week, we simply deny that they exist. Hence children don't have a right to a father and don't need a father. Fathers, are you paying attention? You aren't needed. Walk away right now. Your kids don't need you.

What the House of Commons has explicitly said is that children don't need fathers, or indeed mothers. What they need instead is something called 'supportive parenting'. Therefore, the House of Commons has abolished not only fatherhood, but also motherhood, and replaced both with the gender-neutral, de-sexed, egalitarian and all-inclusive concept of 'parenthood'. Children don't need mothers and fathers, only 'parents'. Who'd have guessed?

What does our government think? Will it continue to surrender to the benighted and ignorant forces of political correctness which are long on intimidation and exceedingly short on common sense and rationality? Or will it explicitly declare itself in favour of mothers and fathers instead of 'parents'?

CHAPTER 20

PARENTS THE BEST JUDGES OF WHAT'S GOOD FOR A CHILD

2008

You want what's best for your child, don't you? Of course you do, we all do, parents, neighbours, relatives, teachers, social workers, the State, everyone. But what happens if you and the State, or some agent of the State, disagree over what is best for your child? Answer: trouble.

We don't know yet whether or not we're to have a referendum on children's rights. The government, having promised one, now looks like it's having second thoughts and will opt for the legislative route instead. This isn't good enough for either child welfare groups such as Barnardos, or for Fine Gael, however. As they repeated again this week, both believe that without a constitutional amendment, children's right won't be properly protected.

But whichever way we go, the topic that will generate the most controversy by far is who gets to decide what is in a child's best interests.

However, let's be clear first of all about what isn't controversial. What isn't controversial is the concept of a child's best interests itself. Of course a child's best interests must be taken into account in all decisions affecting him or her.

What is also uncontroversial is that the State should be allowed to take over the role of parents when parents abuse or neglect their children. That power already exists.

But what is extremely controversial is the notion that the State should be allowed to take over the role of parents when the parents are guilty of neither abuse nor neglect, but merely when a State employee with the power of family intervention thinks they know better than the parents what is in a child's best interests.

There was a very dramatic example of this in Canada recently. The case involved a separated father who had been granted custody of his 12-year-old daughter. He had refused to let her go on a school trip for chatting on websites he disapproves of, and also because she had posted images of herself online which he deemed "inappropriate".

The girl objected, the lawyer appointed to represent her interests after the parents' separation intervened, and the father was taken to court. The court found in favour of the girl on the basis that the punishment was too severe.

Do you think the State should have the power to quash parental decisions such as this, even if the parents have separated (what's the relevance of that?) and when they disagree about what should happen to their child?

Bear in mind that this girl was neither being abused nor neglected. No fundamental rights were being violated.

In Canada, the state has now taken onto itself unprecedented power to interfere in family life for practically any reason whatsoever and what gives it such power is the concept of a child's best interests. In the case in question, the father decided it was in the child's best interests to ground her. The court disagreed. The court decided it was in her best interests to be able to go on the school trip and that was that.

If the concept of a child's best interests is to be inserted into our Constitution, it must be done in a way that strictly delimits the power of the State. If it is instead inserted in a very open-ended manner, then the way will be paved for a Canadian-type situation in which the State can overrule parents for potentially any reason.

In Canada, the state, *de facto*, has told parents that they must raise children only in ways that find favour with the state and its officials, and if some state official disapproves of what a parent has done, the state can intervene and overrule the parents. It is tantamount to the nationalisation of children.

In other words, the concept of a child's best interest, placed in the hands of the State and without being strictly delimited, will lead to a huge increase in the power of the State. This is anti-freedom, anti-parent, and ultimately anti-child because parents, rather than the State, are the ones who know what is in their child's best interests in the vast majority of cases. And even if they don't, or it is in doubt, it is usually a judgement call and certainly not grounds for State intervention.

What the likes of Barnardos and Fine Gael need to make crystal clear is how exactly they will delimit the power of the State if the concept of a child's best interests is placed in the Constitution. They must do this in order to ensure that a Canadian-style situation does not arise here and to ensure the State can only override parents in extreme situations.

They must make very clear what they mean by a child's 'best interests' and also how much power they think the State should be given to decide this. We should not hear another word from them until they have done so.

CHAPTER 21

TEENAGE SEX IS NOT THE NORM, SO WHY DEFEND IT?

2008

Note: This was written following the broadcast of 'The Fairytale of Kathmandu', a documentary about poet Cathal Ó Searcaigh in Kathmandu which raised disturbing questions about sexual exploitation.

If the *Fairytale of Kathmandu* does nothing else, it ought to refocus minds on the thorny subject of the age of consent and encourage us to keep it at 17. We also need to look more closely at transgenerational sex, which is almost always exploitative.

At the heart of the *Fairytale of Kathmandu* is this issue of exploitation rather than homosexuality or heterosexuality *per se*. If Cathal Ó Searcaigh was, say, a middle-aged politician or, even worse, a priest and he was discovered to be having sex with girls of 16 and 17 in some far-flung Third World country, there would also be outrage.

The politician or priest would have no defenders, no enablers, whatsoever. Why does Ó Searcaigh have defenders? Suffice it to say that the defence of Ó Searcaigh by Aosdana (the State-funded artists' organisation) looks an awful lot like an artistic version of clericalism.

But the age of consent issue is an additional, crucial factor in this tale and it can be related to proposals to restore the zone of absolute protection around minors that are contained in the planned children's rights amendment.

Peter Tatchell advocated lowering the age of consent to 14 based on the bizarre notion that this would protect minors against sexual predators – when it would obviously make them even more vulnerable.

In fact, the age of consent could in practice be even lower if Tatchell ever got his way. Another of his proposals is that two people, of apparently any age, should be allowed to have sex so long as they both consent and the age gap between those under the age of 14 is no more than three years.

To spell this out, it would seem to mean that if a 10-year-old had sex with a 13-year-old they would not be in breach of the law so long as they both 'consented' to it.

This is extraordinary, but there is a good prospect that someday it will be the sexual regime in Ireland because what sexual radicals demand today we often grant tomorrow.

The poet Alexander Pope was spot on when he wrote all those years ago: "Vice is a monster of so frightful mien, As to be hated needs but to be seen; Yet seen too oft, familiar with her face, we first endure, then pity, then embrace."

If, on the other hand, we don't want a future in which 50-year-old men and women are free to have sex with teenage boys and girls, now is the time to think long and hard about the direction in which we are headed.

Sexual radicals usually advance their agenda in two ways that have proven to be fantastically effective. The first is to accuse their opponents of being old-fashioned and reactionary and the second is to tell the general public that we must be 'realistic'.

What they mean by 'realistic' is that we must face up to the fact that teenagers have sex, with or without the age of consent. Many, albeit a minority, have sex before they are 17.

What the sexual 'realists' tell us is that we must lower the age of consent in recognition of this and also expand the scope and ambition of sex education.

What they don't tell us is how their strategy is in fact entirely, and possibly willingly, defeatist. For a start, it treats teenagers who have sex before the age of consent as the norm, when not having sex before the age of consent is actually the norm.

But if we are to keep on lowering the age of consent in response to the fact that some teenagers, and even children, are having sex, when do we stop lowering it? At 15, 14, 12? Do we never try to draw a line in the sand?

Instead of lowering the age of consent we need to hold it at 17. In addition, the type of sex education we teach must, at the very least, be aimed at increasing the average age of first sexual intercourse, although even that is hardly very ambitious.

Finally, there is the problem of transgenerational sex. The *Fairytale of Kathmandu* highlighted how sex between much older and much younger people is almost unavoidably exploitative and is doubly so when the older person has money and the younger person has none.

Restoring absolute liability in cases where an adult has sex with a minor would massively discourage this kind of exploitation, especially if the age of consent is held at 17.

Failing this, there should be an age gap of no more than three or four years between a teenager and his or her sexual partner.

Finally, there must be complete societal disapproval of such relationships and none of the 'sophisticated' moral ambiguity that has attended the present case that is in the public eye.

CHAPTER 22

TIME TO GET THE FULL PICTURE ON VOCATIONS

2008

The vocations crisis facing the Catholic Church in Ireland is now so bad even *The Times* in Britain has cottoned on to it. It carried a report about the crisis, or rather the catastrophe, on Wednesday. What a come-down for Mother Church. Ireland once had the highest number of vocations of any country in the world. Today, nowhere is worse. We are the blackspot of blackspots.

Before getting too carried away however, let's acquaint ourselves with a few facts. Here's the most important one. Worldwide, vocations are up. Yes, you read that right. Over the last 30 years they have climbed a rather impressive 70%. Crisis, what crisis? There might be a crisis here, but throughout most of the Catholic world they don't even know the meaning of the word.

Of course, most of those vocations are outside the West. They are to be found in Africa, South America, and Asia. But there are also plenty of vocations in much of Eastern Europe, with the inevitable Poland at the forefront. You might put this down to sociopolitical economics factors rather than spiritual ones and you'd be (sort of) right. But then you could put our abysmal situation down to those same factors. At the moment they're working against the Church, but maybe in the future they won't.

However, even in the West there are some bright spots. Remember, nowhere is worse than Ireland. There are places as bad, but nowhere worse. It's important to say this because we're a parochial lot who think our experience in these matters is universal. It isn't. Not by a long stretch. Dioceses like Madrid, Paris, Sydney, Perth, parts of Italy are all doing relatively well. I stress 'relatively'. Obviously they have fewer vocations than a few decades ago but compared with here, or even with the very recent past, they're not doing too badly at all.

Here's another thing. Vocations go up and down. Between the time of independence and the 1960s, vocations were higher than they were in the 19th Century. I doubt if they'll ever go back to what they were in the middle part of the last century, but I also doubt very much if they'll remain as low as they are today.

At this point the usual cast of characters enter the scene insisting that the answer to the problem is married priests. This is a bit like telling a world-wide company that it needs to change an otherwise successful business plan because of failure in a given market. Why should the Catholic Church change its rule on married clergy when vocations are up, and up in a big way, in most parts of the world? It makes no sense.

In addition, it wouldn't solve the vocations crisis here. While it would ease it somewhat it wouldn't come even close to meeting the basic need of one priest per parish in the future. In the present climate it's very hard to see what would achieve that.

If married priests were the answer, then we would expect that Churches with married clergy would be awash with vocations. But that is far from being the case. The Church of Ireland, for example, is doing considerably better than the Catholic Church in Ireland but not nearly as well as 40 or 50 years ago.

In any event, a married clergy have intrinsic problems of their own. In Britain, for example, married clergy are almost as likely to divorce as the rest of the population. This is partly because of the peculiar pressures of the clerical life, married or not. Children of clergy often hate having to be paragons of virtue in their parishes and rebel. The divorced wives of clergy can find themselves in very difficult financial circumstances because the house in which they lived with their husband is parochial property and does not belong to them.

In addition, a married cleric with a family has a lot less of one very valuable commodity compared with his celibate counterparts – time. The rule of celibacy is intended mainly to make a priest or religious more available for service. We forget that celibacy has a positive side.

The vocations crisis in Ireland and in other parts of the Western world – notwithstanding the bright spots – is not the result of celibacy. The difficulty the other Churches have in attracting vocations is proof of that. The three biggest causes are secularisation, the decline in family size, and a generalised crisis of commitment across the whole of society.

One thing the Church certainly must do is put much, much more effort into promoting vocations. It ploughs far too much money into maintaining its buildings and not nearly enough into promoting the priesthood and religious life. It needs to put serious amounts of time, money and effort into explaining to people what the priesthood is, and why it is valuable and fulfilling. If it can't or won't do this, then it shouldn't be surprised if the priest goes the way of the druid.

CHAPTER 23

WRONG TO BLAME CONSTITUTION FOR FAILURE TO PROTECT CHILDREN

2008

A child abuse case of horrific proportions has plunged Britain into one of its periodic bouts of soul-searching this week.

The case involves an infant known simply as 'Baby P'. He died in August last year, aged just 17 months, following endless physical abuse by his mother's boyfriend – a collector of Nazi memorabilia – and, apparently, her lodger as well.

In Ireland, we have had, and still have, our fair share of child abuse cases. Obviously, there has been abuse of children by clerics. But there has also been abuse of children by their own families.

The most famous examples of the latter are the Kelly Fitzgerald case and the Kilkenny incest case. Kelly Fitzgerald died in 1993, aged 12, following years of neglect and abuse by her parents. The girl in the Kilkenny incest case was continually assaulted and raped by her father between 1976 and 1991.

Both of those cases caused our own bouts of soul-searching. The finger of blame was obviously pointed at the parents. But it was also pointed at social services for failing the girls. Finally, it was pointed at Irish society itself, and, more precisely, at the sort of 'traditional values' that apparently discouraged anyone, including the local community, from intervening to save the girls from harm.

The Kilkenny incest case resulted in a landmark report. In that report, Judge Catherine McGuinness famously blamed the case, in part at least, on the Irish Constitution.

She declared that "the very high emphasis on the rights of the family in the Constitution may consciously, or unconsciously, be interpreted as giving a higher value to the rights of parents than to the rights of children". She went on to recommend the amendment of the Constitution to include "a specific and overt declaration of the rights of born children".

Ever since, those pressing for such an amendment have used the McGuinness line. For example, in April 2005, the Ombudsman for Children, Emily Logan, said that the Kilkenny incest case highlighted the need to change the Constitution.

The trouble with this line of reasoning is that it doesn't even begin to make sense.

The Constitution already allows for intervention where a child is being abused or neglected. The law, therefore, allowed social services to intervene in both the Kelly Fitzgerald case and the Kilkenny incest case. If they failed to do so adequately, then that was their fault and not the Constitution's.

A fall-back position is, of course, that it wasn't so much the Constitution that was to blame, as a set of conservative social attitudes that makes neighbours and professionals reluctant to interfere in family life. This is what Judge McGuinness meant by people 'unconsciously' deferring to the fact that the Constitution seems to prefer parents over children.

But this doesn't work either. For starters, and as Justice Adrian Hardiman pointed out in the 'Baby Ann' case, the Constitution doesn't prefer parents over children, it prefers them over some third parties such as the Church or the State.

But even more to the point, if traditional social attitudes were to blame for the Fitzgerald and Kilkenny cases, then what explains Baby P and other British abuse cases?

The main culprit in the death of this child was his mother's boyfriend. From November 2006 through to Baby P's death in August 2007, he continually abused the child.

Baby P was seen 22 times by social services, 14 times by hospital staff, 13 times by doctors and four times in clinics. Despite this, he was never taken permanently into care. If he had been, he would still be alive.

Why not? Was it because Britain has a constitution which 'prefers parents over children'? No, because Britain doesn't have a written constitution, much less a conservative one.

Was it conservative social attitudes then? No, because much of Britain is shot through with a political correctness that is at war with traditional values. This is especially so in the case of state services. These services have plenty of power of intervention. So, what was to blame then?

Maybe it was simple bureaucratic incompetence combined with a reluctance to be seen to be 'victimising' poor people.

British social commentators, like Melanie Philips, know exactly where to point the blame and they point it in completely the opposite direction than people such as Emily Logan or Judge McGuinness. They point it at the decline of traditional values rather than at their alleged strength.

They point out, correctly, that a vast underclass has been created in Britain by poverty, and by the decline of marriage and traditional morality and that this places ever more children at risk of abuse because the safest place for a child to be, proportionately speaking, is in the married family.

Baby P, and other cases like it, show that abuse happens in all societies. It also shows that attempts to blame Irish abuse cases on traditional morality and the Constitution are blinkered, ideologically self-serving and very wide of the mark.

CHAPTER 24

GANDHI AND POPE PAUL UNITED BY OPPOSITION TO BIRTH CONTROL

2008

Note: Humanae Vitae, *the controversial papal encyclical which reiterated the Church's opposition to artificial birth control, was published in 1968. This column was written to coincide with its 40th anniversary.*

Here is your starter question for ten points. In 1972, which court convicted a man for handing out a contraceptive device to students at a lecture about contraception? Answer: the Massachusetts Superior Court, later confirmed by the State Supreme Judicial Court.

How is this possible? Isn't Massachusetts the most liberal state in America and hadn't the US Supreme Court quashed Connecticut's ban on contraception five years earlier? Maybe some kind of residual Catholic influence was at work, what with all those Irish Catholics in Boston.

For 20 points, who described contraception as "an unforgiveable crime"? Answer: John Calvin.

Martin Luther condemned the use of contraception as worse than incest or adultery.

How is that possible? Haven't Protestants always approved of contraception?

It seems not, but we can still rest easy because Calvin and Luther lived hundreds of years ago.

But wait, just 100 years ago the Lambeth Conference of Anglican leaders described contraception as "demoralising to character and hostile to national welfare".

So even in recent times, Protestants have opposed contraception.

Very well then, what about those nice Hindus the Beatles used to visit?

Sorry to disappoint, but here are the sorts of things they were saying back in the 1920s and 30s: Contraception is "detrimental to the spiritual progress of the human family"; it is "an insult to womanhood"; "any large use of the methods is likely to result in the dissolution of the marriage bond and in free love... birth control to me is a dismal abyss".

And it wasn't just any old Hindu who said these things. Instead, it was the most admired Indian of our times, the Nelson Mandela of his day, none other than Mahatma Gandhi himself.

Et tu Gandhi?

Now, why in the world am I bringing up all this old stuff? The answer is that this very day is the exact 40th anniversary of the promulgation of *Humanae Vitae*, the papal encyclical that reiterated the Church's age-old ban on artificial contraception. This is the encyclical which supposedly saw the Catholic Church definitively take its leave of the modern world and which caused ordinary Catholics to lose faith in its teaching authority.

It's as well to remind ourselves, therefore, that opposition to artificial contraception wasn't peculiarly Catholic, or Christian, or necessarily even religious and that arguments against it could be made without any reference at all to God.

The Massachusetts case quoted above is a good example. By 1972, the State of Massachusetts was no longer in the grip of the Catholic Church. But of course, it never was. This is the home of Harvard University and the ultra-liberal Unitarians. The reason it convicted the man in that case is because it believed that making contraception widely available was harmful to the greater good.

The reason it was still possible for the Superior Court of Massachusetts to do this, even after the US Supreme Court had quashed Connecticut's blanket ban on contraceptives, is because that decision did not outlaw placing some restrictions on their availability.

In fact, as late as the 1960s, two-thirds of American states still placed restrictions on the sale of contraceptives and those laws were only dropped as a result of rapidly changing sexual norms.

Was Gandhi wrong about what the consequences of widely-available contraception would be? Was Pope Paul VI?

Judge for yourself.

Both men predicted that there would be a huge increase in marital infidelity, and there was. Of course there was.

Forgetting for a moment the Catholic Church's blanket opposition to contraceptives, the fear of people like Gandhi, and many Protestants, was that making them freely available to unmarried people would lead to a huge increase in sex outside marriage and, therefore, to marital infidelity.

Both men also predicted it would lead to a lessening of respect for women by men. Certainly, trust between the sexes has been hugely eroded and, if surveys and endless anecdotal evidence are to be believed, women in particular complain that many men are only interested in them for sex.

One thing is certain, however: freely available contraception means it is much easier to have sex with someone you don't know and who doesn't care for you, meaning the exposure to emotional exploitation is huge.

As for the notion that in an age of widely available contraception every child would be a 'wanted child', we now know that this is baloney.

Once you separate sex from love, marriage, commitment and children, when a pregnancy does result, it will be seen as a huge inconvenience, hence the massive rise in abortion and the huge numbers of fathers who want little or nothing to do with their children.

So condemn *Humanae Vitae* if you will.

Laugh at it if you will.

But read it, and then look at the evidence around you and admit that at the very least it was not entirely wrong.

And if you won't believe Pope Paul, then believe Mahatma Gandhi instead.

CHAPTER 25

YOU CANNOT BLAME AFRICAN AIDS EPIDEMIC ON THE CHURCH

2009

Defending the Church sometimes resembles trying to scale a particularly steep and treacherous mountain, only without climbing ropes or oxygen canisters. To make matters worse, the Church itself often conspires to send avalanches crashing your way.

Just recently, for example, we had decision by the Pope to lift the excommunication of four anti-Vatican II bishops, including one who effectively denied the Holocaust, although the Pope did not know about that.

Having lifted that excommunication, we then learnt that a Brazilian bishop had declared that the mother of a raped nine-year-old girl had been automatically excommunicated because she had facilitated the aborting of her daughter's twins.

At times like that, you simply try to get out of the way or else you agree with the Church's critics when they are right, as they sometimes are.

But at other times you feel obliged to defend the Church because you believe it is being unjustly attacked.

This week, Pope Benedict has been in Africa. Africa is, of course, the epicentre of the HIV/AIDS crisis. The Catholic Church is opposed to condom use as part of the fight against HIV/AIDS and stands accused of causing millions of deaths even though it provides treatment and love and care to countless numbers of HIV/AIDS sufferers.

When asked just prior to his departure for Africa to comment on the Church's teaching on condoms, the Pope stuck to his guns. Not only that, he blamed condoms for contributing to the very problem they are supposed to solve. Cue outrage. Even the French government has become involved.

In Africa, or more precisely in sub-Saharan Africa, there are estimated to be roughly 27 million people infected with HIV/AIDS. A further 25 million have already died.

Is it fair to blame millions of AIDS deaths on the Church? In truth, only the Church's most extreme critics would do that, although there are plenty of them, and there are lots more who uncritically believe the critics.

But here are a few facts for the uncritical to consider. Fact one is that only around 20% of non-Muslim Africans are Catholic. This means the other 80% aren't listening to the Church, even theoretically, and so are not susceptible to its anti-condom message.

In turn this means that even if the Church was responsible for every death by AIDS of every infected African Catholic - and it isn't, even remotely - the vast majority of deaths cannot be laid at its door. Fact two is that Catholics who have sex outside marriage are already disobeying the Church. Why would they then turn around and obey its anti-condom edict? It makes no sense.

On the other hand, a Catholic who obeys the Church about condoms is also very likely to obey it with regard to sexual morality in general. If they and their spouse are doing that, there is no chance of them contracting HIV/AIDS, short of receiving an infected blood transfusion. The more intelligent critics of the Church will concede this point, but then dismiss Catholic sexual morality in any case on the grounds that it is unrealistic. This brings us to the final and most important point, which is that condom promotion in Africa is a miserable failure.

It is this which fails the realism test. It has been tried for years and the rate of infection has kept rising

It has only fallen in those countries which promote sexual fidelity. The very best book on this subject is called *The Invisible Cure* by Helen Epstein. She has no axe to grind for the Catholic Church but she cites irrefutable evidence which shows that fidelity programmes are the most effective way of combating HIV/AIDS.

Epstein shows that the UN ignored reports, which it had itself commissioned, confirming the effectiveness of fidelity programmes. This is an immense scandal deserving of condemnation by governments which are instead directing their ire at the Pope.

Then, in one very telling passage, Epstein quotes a pro-condom activist who confesses why people such as himself ignored the evidence about fidelity programmes.

He says: "There was a sense that promoting fidelity must be totally wrong if it was a message favoured by the Christian right. We've made an emotional set of decisions and people have suffered terribly because of that. Everything we learn about the epidemic goes in slowly and is resisted on the way."

This devastating admission means that Africans are dying not because of Church opposition to condom programmes, but because of Western aid agencies and Governments and their blinkered, dogmatic, anti-religious opposition to fidelity programmes.

This is the exact opposite of what we are led to believe and any development worker, journalist, or politician who continues to disregard the fact that fidelity programmes work is part of the problem, not the solution. So let them open their minds to what the evidence actually has to say instead of engaging in cheap, knee-jerk anti-Catholicism.

CHAPTER 26

SAYING NEVER AGAIN MEANS LITTLE UNLESS WE FIND OUT WHY

2009

*Note: This column was written in response to the
publication of the Ryan Report which investigated abuse
in industrial schools and other institutions.*

For practising Catholics there is only one appropriate response to the report of the Child Abuse Commission, and it is one of deep, unadulterated shame. How can this have happened? How can priests and religious, charged with upholding the Gospel, have so utterly betrayed that Gospel?

Let's not doubt that there have been thousands of priests, nuns and brothers down all the decades who have done heroic work helping the poor and the outcast. I think, for example, of Fr Thomas Carroll of St Andrew's Church on Westland Row who died of cholera 150 years ago while ministering to victims of that same disease in inner city Dublin.

Now the danger is that his work, and the work of all those others like him, will be overshadowed, perhaps even forgotten and expunged, as a result of the great evil perpetrated by other priests and religious.

To repeat, how can this have happened?

The overwhelming reason is that certain individuals, not fit to look after animals, were instead given the care of children.

We now know that child abusers are attracted to institutions and professions where they can gain trusted and privileged access to children. In Ireland, until recently, no institution was more trusted or more privileged than the Catholic Church.

Why else did it happen?

It happened because no one blew the whistle.

Even when orders knew about sexual abuse, no one in authority thought to tell the relevant authorities. The first instinct of all institutions confronted by a scandal is to cover it up. This is never excusable. It is doubly inexcusable when the organisation in question is a religious one.

Another factor at work was the ultra-authoritarian temper of the times. This does not explain the sex abuse but it does explain the physical abuse and the regimes of very harsh discipline that usually prevailed in the industrial schools and other children's homes.

The Ryan Report throws its net wider than simply the Catholic Church. It looks at Marlborough House, for example. This was a detention centre run exclusively by the State and it was also infected by the terrible authoritarianism of the time. Physical abuse was widespread. Sexual abuse also occurred.

It looks at children's homes, most of which were run by the Catholic Church but some of which were run by other bodies. The children's homes were also terrible places and many of the abusers were lay people.

In fact, the Commission looks at 161 settings other than industrial schools, including hostels and foster care homes and finds instances of abuse throughout these settings, right down to the present day – no matter who ran them, or runs them.

The report engages in no systematic comparison of our industrial school system with Britain's industrial school system.

We know abuses happened there too. But was ours worse? How much worse? Why?

What was our system like compared with Sweden, Germany and Switzerland where the industrial schools originated?

Was there a better response in the 19th Century to the problem of thousands upon thousands of street children of the sort famously depicted in the novels of Charles Dickens?

What about the ISPCC? A third of those who testified to the Investigation Committee of the Ryan Commission were placed in industrial schools as a result of a recommendation by the ISPCC.

Were these recommendations justified? Was the ISPCC over zealous?

An extremely bland press release by the ISPCC in response to the report throws no light on the issue.

Were Catholic-run institutions worse than institutions run by others organisations around the world, including the State?

As a Catholic I would dearly love to know the answer to this.

If they were worse, then we need to look into the nature of the Catholic Church itself to find an explanation.

A further question; were institutions run by Irish priests and religious – whether here or abroad – worse than similar institutions run by, say, Italian priests and religious?

Where do we go from here? We have already had apologies aplenty from both the State and the 18 orders that ran these institutions.

A redress board has paid out more than €140m in compensation. Helplines have been established.

Psychiatric care is paid for. Some of the perpetrators have been imprisoned.

Many of Ryan's recommendations actually deal with the present, not the past.

Justice Ryan and his colleagues want to ensure that our childcare system is run to the highest possible standard.

We know that it is not.

We know that the State's child protection policy, Children First, is not properly implemented.

The best response to this report is to continue bringing justice, healing and reconciliation to the victims of past child abuse, but it is also to bring the present system up to the standard demanded by Sean Ryan in order to protect children currently in care.

This is the only way the words 'Never again' can have any meaning.

CHAPTER 27

OUR DELUSIONS ABOUT SEX ARE AS POWERFUL AS EVER

2009

We've always been deluded about sex. In the past we thought we were sexually pure and happy. Today we think we're sexually liberated and happy.

In his book, *Occasions of Sin*, historian Diarmuid Ferriter uses liberal Ireland's favourite pantomime villain, Archbishop John Charles McQuaid, to show just how deluded we were about sex. In an unpublished writing in 1965 McQuaid said this on the subject: "There is probably a saner attitude to sex in this country than almost anywhere else."

Even then that would have seemed fairly deluded. With the benefit of hindsight, it seems utterly insane.

There were, of course, the terrible abuses taking place in residential institutions that we now know about, but Ferriter also catalogues the sexual crimes were coming before the courts at the time, and the reality of sex outside marriage.

But sex outside marriage wasn't widespread. If it was, there would have been a very high rate of births outside marriage, and there wasn't, even allowing for cover-ups. Therefore, a very great many of those unmarried people were celibate.

In the liberal telling of the story the blame for all this can be laid almost exclusively at the feet of the Church. In fact, two other completely unavoidable factors were mostly to blame; biology and economics.

Nothing much could be done about the biological factor until the invention of the Pill – which created problems of its own. If a woman was having sex she was going to become pregnant. When last I checked that didn't apply to Irish women only. That's why traditional sexual morality was universal and not just an Irish or even a Catholic phenomenon. It's why we, and everyone else as well, tied sex to marriage.

However, if biology explains why we tied sex to marriage, it doesn't explain why we Irish delayed getting married for so long. Ferriter quotes a very telling statistic in this regard to show just how different we used to be in this respect. In 1926 almost three-quarters of men and half of women aged between 25 and 43 were unmarried. Incredible.

But again, this phenomenon had nothing whatever to do with the Church. Economics, not theology, was the driver here. The legacy of the Famine persisted for decades after it. It meant that people wanted to be as economically secure as possible before getting married and this took a long time to achieve.

Therefore, it wasn't the fault of the Church that we weren't living in one giant Playboy Mansion racing to be the first naked person into Hugh Hefner's grotto. The Church simply reinforced a type of sexual morality that made economic and biological sense. It was responding to the facts of life, you might say.

At the same time, however, no one can deny that a lot of Catholic preaching about sex was appallingly and inexcusably anti-body. But then, the Victorians were pretty bad about this as well.

In the liberal telling of the story we're left behind all that sexual repression and are now happily living in the sunny uplands of sexual liberation. This only shows we're as delusional as ever.

Ferriter, to give him his due, acknowledges the all-too-modern problem of the early sexualisation of teenagers, and the huge growth in sexually transmitted diseases.

But the real problem is that we've not only separated sex from marriage, we're now so wedded to personal autonomy that we have separated sex from commitment and from having children until we're often well into our thirties and even beyond. So while we're no longer prudish about sex itself, we're 'prudish' about commitment and we're 'prudish' about children.

DAVID QUINN

Therefore, we delay and delay making commitments until it is some-times too late. Or, in a panic, we settle for someone who's a lot less than ideal. Or someone we hoped would commit to us breaks our heart instead. Or we're left literally holding the baby. Or we decide not to have the baby and opt to abort it instead. Or we delay having children until we're had all our fun and then discover we're 40 and infertile.

On the top of this, the sex revolution has done nothing to reduce sex crimes and has almost certainly increased them to judge from rape figures.

It is any wonder that surveys of men and women show ever growing mutual mistrust between the sexes, and especially that women distrust men more and more? A recent American study showed that women are unhappier now than they were 40 years ago, on both sides of the Atlantic.

John Charles McQuaid may have decided back in 1965 that there is "probably a saner attitude to sex in this country than anywhere else". But today, liberals believe exactly that about 2009, and they're just as wrong as McQuaid was then but for entirely opposite reasons.

The sex revolution has created multiple, as yet unacknowledged prob-lems of its own. On this score, it really is time for liberals to display a little more maturity and a little less self-congratulation.

CHAPTER 28

MARRIAGE BREAKDOWN IS THE BIG LIBERAL BLIND SPOT

2009

To be pro-marriage these days is to be dismissed as an eccentric at best or a bigot at worst. You think I'm exaggerating? Then take heed of the following.

This week, new CSO figures revealed that the number of births taking place outside of marriage keeps on rising. It is now one birth in every three and among 20-24-year olds, it is the majority. But if you point out that this is a cause for alarm, you will be accused of victimising single parents.

Or if you point out that same-sex marriage or civil partnerships are a bad idea, and they are, you are accused of homophobia. If you suggest that the 500% increase in marital breakdown that has occurred since 1986 is a bad thing, you're stigmatising divorced people.

As for cohabitation, well, it's up 400% in only ten years. But on your peril try pointing out that cohabiting couples are more likely to divorce than couples who don't first cohabit, or that cohabiting parents are twice as likely as married parents to split before the children are grown up. Again you're offending people.

The pro-marriage argument is exceedingly simple. It is based on the indisputable fact that it is best, in general, for a child to be raised by a loving mother and father who are married. All counter-arguments must deny this. All counter-arguments must say that there is no special advantage in a child having a loving, married mum and dad.

But in fact, the argument rarely gets this far because it is short-circuited by accusations of judgmentalism, prejudice and even bigotry. Therefore, most people are now scared to defend marriage, scared to say it's best for a child to have a loving mother and father, scared of being labelled.

Politicians are the most scared of all. When is the last time you heard a politician, with one or two honourable exceptions, defend marriage as the best place for kids?

Instead we're told to celebrate 'family diversity', meaning every family should be supported just as much as the married family. Sounds fair enough, doesn't it? Who could be against that? But consider what we are being asked to celebrate.

What we are being asked to celebrate is more and more children not being raised by a married mother and father.

Certainly all families should be treated with respect and there are many good and understandable reasons why a child ends up without a father. All families indeed should be helped.

But to say that every family – cohabiting, single-parent, gay, etc.., - is as beneficial for children as the family based on the marriage between a loving mother and father, is to say something that simply isn't true.

Consider the example of Limerick city where almost 60% of children are born outside of marriage – an astounding figure.

Now consider Moyross. In Moyross, the amount of marital breakdown is roughly three times the national average and only around 40% of families are marital families. There is lots of cohabitation and lots of single-parent families. Practically no other area in Ireland has more 'family diversity'.

The consequences are disastrous. Moyross is caught in a classic vicious circle. Poverty causes family breakdown, and family breakdown causes poverty. In truth, both help to cause crime. Small children in some parts of Limerick city are now being inducted into the criminal gangs and children as young as eight are burning families out of their homes.

Liberals are more than willing to accept the connection between poverty and crime, and other social problems. However, they fiercely resist linking marriage breakdown with social problems and if anyone has the temerity to do so, they are pilloried as prejudiced.

This is a colossal and dangerous blind spot. A refusal to accept that the decline of marriage is very bad for society is similar to the blind spot that had us refusing to accept that we had an enormous property bubble on our hands which resulted in economic calamity.

Worse than that, liberals insist on calling family breakdown 'family diversity'. Instead of lamenting it, they insist on us celebrating it. Only a society that has completely lost is bearings could do such a thing.

In places like Moyross, as elsewhere, 'family diversity' generally means no father. The Chief Superintendent of Limerick, Willie Keane has said the result is that the gangs take the place of the fathers.

Meanwhile, Brendan Dempsey, head of St Vincent de Paul in Cork, says that in parts of Cork city, nine in every 10 homes visited by society members are run by lone parents and there is no dad to be seen. Some children ask him if he will be their daddy. That is simply tragic.

If we fix marriage in areas like Moyross, we are halfway to fixing the problems of Moyross. Promoting marriage would be a much better thing than passing even tougher anti-gang laws such as announced by government this week.

But disastrously, we are too busy disguising family breakdown as 'family diversity' to even consider something as sensible as that.

CHAPTER 29

RELIGIOUS ORDERS ARE NOT ALL
EQUALLY CULPABLE FOR ABUSE

2009

*Note: This column was written in response to the
publication of the Ryan Report which dealt with abuse in
industrial schools and other institutions.*

When government officials met the 18 religious orders dealt with in the Ryan Report, were they aware of a very important finding contained in the report, namely that abuse of all kinds was far more prevalent in some schools than in others? At this stage, the general public probably has the impression that all the institutions and all the religious orders who ran them were as bad as each other. This is simply not the case.

Here are some of the facts and figures taken directly from the Ryan Report that the government ought to know. One of the most striking findings is as follows: four schools (not named) accounted for no fewer than half of all physical abuse complaints against boys' schools heard by the commission. A total of 26 boys' schools had such reports made against them, but in 10 of these an average of 1.8 complaints was heard.

What this means is that a boy was vastly more likely to be abused in the four worst institutions than in the 10 'best'.

Turning to sex abuse in boys' schools we find a similar pattern. As the Ryan Report itself says: "The frequency of sexual abuse reports varied widely between schools."

A total of 242 witnesses reported sex abuse incidents. Twenty boys institutions were reported to the commission concerning sex abuse but four of these accounted for an incredible 61% of all sex abuse reports, while

11 of them accounted for a total of 12% of the reports. The most common form of sex abuse was molestation. Rape accounted for 12% of the cases.

Similar wide variations are found in the institutions run by nuns. The commission heard 383 reports of physical abuse in 39 schools. But three of these schools accounted for more than a third of these complaints, or 48 each, while 19 accounted for an average of 2.5 complaints each.

Sex abuse was much less prevalent in the girls' institutions than in the boys', something the Ryan Report acknowledges. This is to be expected, as men are much more likely than women to be sexual abusers.

We also find from the report (volume III, chapters 7 and 9 to be precise) that a relative handful of priests, nuns and brothers accounted for most of the abuse. For example, while 241 nuns were named as physical abusers, 156 were named by just one person each, while four were named by a total of 125 individuals.

The Ryan Report says, correctly, that 800 people were named as abusers in over 200 institutions. But taken on its own, this is misleading. A proper analysis of the report – which in all fairness should have been highlighted in the executive summary – shows that about half of the 800 were named by just one person each, while a few dozen were named by numerous witnesses.

In addition, a relative handful of the 200 institutions – about 16 – account for a grossly disproportionate share of abuse reports. Those 16 were run by eight of the 18 orders that managed the institutions.

With the exception of Newtownforbes, Co. Longford, the 17 institutions that have their own chapters in the Ryan Report had 20 or more complaints made against them. This is the number it took to trigger a special investigation by the commission. In other words, all the rest of the 200 institutions had fewer than 20 complaints against them.

The commission has confirmed to me that some institutions had either one or no complaint made against them.

What all this means is that the institutions and the orders that ran them were not uniformly as bad as one another. In some of the schools, you were far more likely to be abused than in others.

The Mercy Sisters, for example, ran 26 institutions in all, and all were about the same size. Four of these had 20 or more complaints made against them, meaning 22 did not. A lot seems to have depended on the personality of the person running the institution.

Does the government believe that all of the 18 orders are equally guilty? If it does, then it is badly mistaken.

Take the tiny French order called the Daughters of the Heart of Mary, for example. They ran a place in Dun Laoghaire until 1985 and in its 130-year history, about 2,100 children passed through it.

It received only a handful of abuse allegations. Do this institution and the order that ran it deserve to be put on the same level as, say, Ferryhouse, Clonmel, Co. Tipperary, where Michael O'Brien, who appeared on *Questions and Answers*, was savagely abused?

When dealing with the orders, the government needs to learn the lessons of the Ryan Report in full, and one of those lessons is that there was wide variation between the institutions, and the orders that ran them.

Some were much less abusive than others. The government should not adopt an attitude of 'an equal plague on all your houses' because that would not be true to the facts.

CHAPTER 30

THE 'COMPASSIONATE' THEOLOGY THAT FAILED THE VICTIMS OF ABUSE

2010

Note: The Murphy Report (2009) dealt with abuse in Dublin archdiocese. The following year, a further chapter was released dealing with Tony Walsh, a defrocked priest and one of the worst of the abusers.

The chapter of the Murphy Report on child abuse in the Dublin archdiocese that deals with former priest, Tony Walsh, and was released last week, is revealing in two very important aspects.

First, it makes it utterly clear that a 'compassionate' interpretation of canon law was one of the main factors behind the Church's failure to protect children as these scandals peaked in the 1970s and the 1980s.

Second, it shows how gardaí in the case of Walsh also failed to protect children when they were informed of Walsh's activities in the early 1990s.

It is also worth noting that while Cardinal Desmond Connell does not emerge from this chapter with a completely clean bill of health - gardaí should have been told of the complaints against Walsh as soon as he became aware of them after becoming Archbishop of Dublin in March 1988 – he dealt with Walsh far better than his two immediate predecessors.

In fact, in the Walsh chapter, the Murphy Commission says of Cardinal Connell: "However, the Commission recognises that Archbishop Connell did act decisively once be became archbishop."

In respect of canon law, the most important figure in the Dublin archdiocese during much of the period in question was Msgr Gerard Sheehy, now deceased.

The chapter on Walsh shows how Sheehy was completely resistant to punishing clerical sex offenders under either Church (canon) or civil law.

He was resistant because he believed that child abusers were victims of their impulses and therefore should be treated for their 'illness' instead of being laicised and/or sent to prison.

For example, the chapter mentions a meeting that took place in the diocesan offices in August 1990 at which the possibility of laicising Walsh was discussed. Cardinal Connell, Sheehy, and several of the auxiliary bishops, including Eamonn Walsh, were present.

Following the meeting Sheehy described it as: "probably the most depressing meeting I have ever attended. There was not a single word, from anyone, about the fact that we are dealing with a disordered person. The whole thrust was: 'how best can we get rid of him?'...To crown my depression, Bishop Walsh made the outrageous suggestion that the archbishop [Connell] inform the civil authorities about Fr [Walsh's] homosexual orientation."

Five years later, when the Walsh case was breaking in the media, Msgr Sheehy advised Archbishop Connell (as he was then): "I think it important that every one of us should at this stage avoid any excessive reaction – no matter what the civil law may say. Least of all should we pay any attention to the money-making posturing of the media."

So between 1990 and 1995, Msgr Sheehy's attitude had remained unchanged.

All along he resisted attempts to have Walsh laicised, or 'defrocked'. It is clear also that his attitude towards canon law existed in the Roman Rota, the highest canon law court.

When the Dublin archdiocese decided to laicise Walsh in 1993, Walsh appealed to the rota and the rota quashed the decision instead telling Dublin to restrict him to a monastery for 10 years.

It was only when Archbishop Connell appealed to the Pope via Cardinal Joseph Ratzinger, his trusted advisor, that Walsh was finally dismissed from the priesthood in January 1995.

Msgr Sheehy was surprised by this, regarding it as a "new departure".

But it wasn't. In fact, it was a reversion to the old practice of using canon law – where justified – to punish errant priests.

Archbishop of Dublin Diarmuid Martin has confirmed to Pope Benedict (using the words of the Pope) that "ecclesiastical penal law functioned until the late 1950s".

But as the Murphy Report itself makes clear, from sometime in the 1960s, canon law fell into disuse and disrespect. It was regarded as being too legalistic and against the new spirit of 'compassion' that was supposedly arising in the 1960s.

Msgr Sheehy helped to force this 'compassionate' spirit onto canon law with absolutely disastrous consequences.

Given, on the one hand, the fact that canon law fell into disuse, and on the other hand that, even when used it was interpreted in a 'compassionate' light, we begin to understand why these scandals peaked in the 1970s and 1980s.

Prior to that the Church still failed in its duty to report errant priests to the civil authorities (it wasn't the only body to do so). However, canon law was used often against clerical abusers meaning far fewer children were harmed.

But in the free-for-all atmosphere of the 1970s and 1980s when sex offenders rather than the children they abused were being treated as the real 'victims', the number of cases of abuse soared.

In the US they peaked between 1975 and 1980 and a similar pattern is revealed in the Murphy Report. The 1970s was by far and away the worst decade in the Dublin archdiocese for abuse.

A question that arises from all this is the following: what school of theology was responsible for the 'compassionate' reading or abandonment of canon law?

Finally, turning to the gardaí, they were first informed of allegations against Tony Walsh by the mother of a boy in 1990.

Walsh was in Mellifont Abbey at this point and Mellifont informed the gardaí that "there were numerous allegations of paedophilia against him".

No action was taken by the gardaí.

In August 1991, Fr Willie Walsh (later Bishop Walsh) called into Whitehall Garda station and told them that the Church was investigating allegations against Tony Walsh.

Again, no action was taken by the gardaí.

Then, in early 1992 following Tony Walsh's return to Ireland from another stint in the UK in a clinic, Msgr Alex Stenson said to a garda sergeant: "In view of Fr [Walsh's] behaviour in the past you might give this information whatever attention you think it may require."

Again, nothing was done. In fact, no action was taken by the gardaí until the mid-1990s when the media began to report Walsh's actions.

So the victims of Tony Walsh were failed both by Church and State. They were failed by a combination of inaction, a desire to avoid scandal, and a flawed theology.

CHAPTER 31

COHABITING COUPLES FACE A RUDE AWAKENING WHEN NEW LEGISLATION FORCES THEM TO 'MARRY'

2010

Note: Aside from giving legal protections to same-sex couples, the Civil Partnership Act also gave marriage-like rights to cohabiting couples.

Are you cohabiting? If so, the law will shortly be knocking at your door thanks to the upcoming *Civil Partnership Bill*. So far, what little debate there has been about this extremely significant piece of legislation has focussed almost entirely on what it will mean for gay and lesbian couples. Almost no attention whatsoever has been paid to how it is going to affect the country's 121,000 cohabiting couples.

The bill was at committee stage in the Dáil this week. Once it becomes law in the coming months any cohabiting couple that has been together for three or more years, two years if they have children, will find themselves caught in a legal web not of their own making.

The bill will allow one partner to sue the other for maintenance and a property settlement in the event of a break-up.

Now, most people cohabit precisely to avoid legal entanglements of this sort. These days what 'living in sin' really means is living outside a legal framework. It's getting married that puts you inside a legal framework with its rights and obligations and protections.

What the government is proposing is effectively the abolition of co-habitation as we have always known it. Why is it doing this? The cynical view is that family lawyers have cooked up another way to make money for themselves.

The less cynical view is that it is a response to the reality that there are now so many cohabiting couples in the country.

Back in 1996, there were only 31,000 cohabiting couples in Ireland but by 2006 this had jumped to 121,000 – a truly stupendous increase in a short time. Ireland now has a higher rate of cohabitation than the US, and it's only somewhat behind Britain.

So, given the reality of cohabitation, shouldn't cohabiting couples be given some of the same rights and protections as married couples?

Actually, there are several arguments against what the government is proposing. One is that it undermines marriage, another is that it is an attack on personal autonomy and choice. The first argument says that the more you provide legally-protected alternatives to marriage, the more you undermine marriage. If people can obtain the protections of marriage by cohabiting, the incentive to marry is reduced.

Is this a bad thing? Emphatically yes, especially for children because marriage is much more stable than cohabitation. For example, the British Millennium Cohort Study shows that only 35% of children born into a cohabiting union will live with both of their parents throughout their childhood, compared with 70% of children born to married couples.

But even if you couldn't care less about marriage there is still the personal autonomy argument which is that people should be allowed to live together if that's what they want without being forced into a legal relationship after three years.

Of course, the government can respond that people can opt out of having this legal relationship imposed on them by the new law if they want. But how many cohabiting couples will know they have to do this?

And why should they have to? Why should they have to go near a lawyer and pay the lawyer to draw up some kind of opt-out contract?

In any case, there is almost no demand for this new law as it relates to cohabitation. Practically no one, bar some family lawyers, has asked for it.

One reason for this lack of demand is that most cohabiting couples end up getting married. That is, cohabitation isn't an alternative to marriage, it's a prelude. The rest usually break up in pretty short order.

In fact, another British study shows that only 3% of cohabiting relationships last more than ten years.

The final government argument in favour of this measure is actually more subtle and somewhat more compelling. It is that in some cohabiting relationships one person wants to get married and the other doesn't but they find it hard to leave the relationship because they have become financially dependent on their partner.

Therefore, it is argued, such individuals should be given the right to apply for maintenance and a property settlement in the event of a break-up.

Let's concede this point then, because it's not a bad one. So, is there a way to cater for it that respects both marriage and personal autonomy? I think there is.

I think the way to do it is to provide the protection this bill envisages but after seven years or so, not three.

It probably takes about this length of time for a condition of financial dependency to properly develop in a cohabiting relationship, but the fact that most cohabiting couples will have broken up or got married before then protects both marriage and personal autonomy.

Will the government accept such an amendment? Not on your life because when it comes to this bill the government is deaf, dumb and blind to all common sense.

Cohabiting couples are in for a rude awakening.

CHAPTER 32

NO POPE HERE!

2010

*Note: This was written as Pope Benedict XVI arrived in
Britain. Contrary to predictions, this visit was a big success.
Beforehand, the Pope was subjected to enormous criticism.*

Ian Paisley is in Scotland, protesting against the Pope's visit. No surprise
there. We all know that Paisley is a rabid anti-Catholic of longstanding, so
what else would you expect?

But Paisley is a throw-back. His hard-line anti-Catholic Protestantism
hardly exists in Britain any more and is fading even in the North. But it is being replaced by something else. Instead of Protestant anti-Catholicism, we
now have secular anti-Catholicism.

The modern successors to Ian Paisley are militant atheists, such as Richard
Dawkins and Christopher Hitchens, and militant gay activists like Peter Tatchell.
Their contempt for Catholicism (and all orthodox religion) knows no bounds.

Tatchell's programme on the Church the other night on Channel 4 was
a model of one-sidedness, a piece of propaganda worthy of Michael Moore's
Fahrenheit 9/11.

A couple of weeks before, the station gave Richard Dawkins a wad of cash
to take aim at faith-based schools. The usual hatchet job ensued.

Of course, Dawkins, Hitchens and Tatchell would recoil from the idea
that they are in the least like Ian Paisley. They would imagine that they are
his opposites in every way.

But while the sources of their complaints against the Catholic Church
would differ from Paisley (he bases his attacks on his interpretation of the

Bible, whereas most of their complaints revolve around sex), you'd be hard put to say which one loathes the Church more.

The sheer hatred that some secular commentators are displaying towards the Church has completely lost contact with reason and moderation.

Writing in the London *Independent* last week, Julie Burchill, in the course of a generalised screed against the Pope, managed to bring in Wayne Rooney's liking for prostitutes and said he "had been acting exactly as Catholic men are expected to - choosing one sort of woman to marry and another to have sex with".

So there you have it. Catholic men visit prostitutes because their Church hypocritically encourages them to do so.

How do you top this? What Burchill has written about Catholics is the modern-day equivalent of *Punch* magazine's merciless and notorious caricaturing of the Irish back in the 19th Century. For good measure, her piece was accompanied by a cartoon of the Pope that depicted him as a vampire-like creature. *Punch* would definitely have been proud.

Although John Paul II visited Britain in 1982, this is actually the first state visit by a Pope to Britain since the Reformation. Now we know why it has been so hard for the British state to issue an invitation to a Pope - it remains the home of a very rabid form of anti-Catholicism.

How would the Pope be received if he was invited to Ireland? We could expect the same ultra-hostile reaction from secular opinion here.

If secular anti-Catholicism in Britain can be compared with old-style Protestant anti-Catholicism, here, the comparison is more with anti-English ultra-nationalism.

As we know, no reigning British monarch has come to Ireland since independence almost 90 years ago and we still don't know if or when Queen Elizabeth II will come.

She has not been able to come because we fear the kind of anti-English feeling it might provoke. Anti-English sentiment is obviously fading fast but if she had come here in, say, 1985, republicans would have taken to the streets in numbers.

Today, we pat ourselves on the back because a visit by the Queen is far more likely than it once was. We praise ourselves for our growing 'maturity'.

But many of the same people who want the Queen to come here and who decry crude, anti-English nationalism are the very ones most guilty - in the name of 'liberalism' - of the crudest anti-Catholicism.

Should this Pope come here soon, they will go into overdrive to stir up public feeling against him, just as nationalists did when Queen Victoria came here in 1900.

She was then called 'the Famine Queen'. Benedict will be the 'protector of child abusers' (and he is nothing of the sort).

The upsurge in anti-religious feeling in the Western world was sparked by the election of George Bush in 2000 and the September 11 attacks.

Of course, the scandals are also to blame for the explosion of anti-Catholic feeling. But as Ed Koch, the liberal, Jewish former mayor of New York said a few months ago, they are being used as an opportunity to bring down the Church because of its opposition to abortion, its support for traditional sexual morality, its male-only priesthood and so on.

Although most Britons don't care about the Pope's visit one way or the other - nevertheless, sizable crowds lined the streets for him in Edinburgh city centre yesterday - such is the din created by his critics that the background noise to his visit is the worst of any country that he has visited to date.

But if he came to Ireland in the present climate, it would be at least as bad because over here contempt for Catholicism has replaced hatred of England in certain quarters.

The one-eyed secularist rules and his cry is Paisley's one: 'No Pope here!'

CHAPTER 33

RTÉ TOOK MAJOR INTEREST IN MINOR MASS BOYCOTT

2010

If a single solitary person was to call on people to boycott RTÉ on a given day of the week in protest against, say, its perceived bias, how do you imagine RTÉ would react? I'd imagine they'd ignore the call completely and among themselves dismiss the person as a crank.

But when a single solitary person has the Catholic Church in his or her sights, it's a different matter entirely. Then the person gets all the publicity they can handle. This is exactly what happened to Jennifer Sleeman when she called on Catholics to boycott Masses last Sunday in protest against the male-only priesthood.

In the event, the call for the boycott was a total damp squib. There was no measurable effect on Mass attendance and some priests said that, if anything, attendance was up. Nonetheless, RTÉ covered the event as though it wasn't a total failure.

On Sunday night, its television news programme interviewed random Mass-goers who wanted nothing to do with the boycott. To 'balance' them it then interviewed specifically selected individuals, including Professor Linda Hogan, a long-time supporter of women priests and all things liberal.

We might ask how would RTÉ react if on 'Boycott RTÉ Day', there was no discernible drop in its viewership figures, but nevertheless TV3 went out of its way to give the impression that something of note had really taken place? Without doubt, RTÉ would see it is a piece of anti-RTÉ campaigning by TV3.

To add insult to injury, RTÉ then gave yet more coverage to the 'boycott' on Monday night. This time it interviewed Fr Tony Flannery of the newly founded 'Association of Catholic Priests'.

The Association had attacked the bishops' statement on the matter as "unhelpful", accused it of "bordering on triumphalism" and claimed that there had been "substantial support" for the boycott without offering any evidence for the claim.

The Monday night report said that while there hadn't been "universal" support for the boycott - are we supposed to believe there was *almost* universal support? - "some Mass-goers had worn the green armband in solidarity". So once again RTÉ was equating the huge numbers who went to Mass as usual on Sunday with the miniscule number who supported Mrs Sleeman.

In fact, the report was perfect from RTÉ's point of view because it allowed it once again to air the liberal position re women in the Church and at the same time give publicity to an organisation that should be renamed 'Priests for Liberal Reform in the Church'.

The boycott was always unlikely to succeed because most Catholics will never use the Mass as a political weapon. But Mrs Sleeman achieved her aim in one respect, in that she got people talking about the issue of women's ordination.

However, what she also highlighted was the need for the Irish Church to explain Catholic teaching on this matter. It needs to explain, for example, that the male-only priesthood is linked to the nature of the Mass itself and specifically the act of Consecration. Jesus' maleness was no more accidental than his choice of bread to represent his body and wine to represent his blood.

None of these elements of the Mass can be changed without calling into question whether a valid act of Consecration would take place at all.

Of course, you may think this is all hocus pocus anyway, but if so then you're rejecting the core sacred act of the Catholic faith, in which case why ordain anyone, because if no act of Consecration takes place no matter what, then we don't need an ordained priesthood.

In any event, in the last two weeks we have seen RTÉ doing its best to talk down the visit of the Pope to the UK, and talk up the boycott of the Mass. One could be forgiven for thinking it wanted the former to fail and the latter to succeed.

But course, that's just me being paranoid - as everyone knows, RTÉ is a model of objectivity in all things.

CHAPTER 34

OUR DEBT TO CHRISTIANITY
IS FAR GREATER THAN WE THINK

2011

A few days ago as part of his Christmas schedule, Pope Benedict XVI visited a prison in Rome to decry overcrowding and assure the inmates that no matter what they had done, they are worthy of respect and dignity.

The Pope received a rapturous welcome from the prisoners, many of whom were visibly moved by the occasion.

This practice of visiting prisoners goes right back to the start of Christianity. It is a response to the words of Jesus to his followers: "I was naked and you clothed me, I was sick and you came to me, I was in prison and you visited me."

Prior to Christianity, there was no tradition in the West of seeing prisoners as people deserving of respect and dignity, as people we should be willing to visit even if they are total strangers who may have done terrible things.

This is only one of many ways in which Christianity transformed the western moral imagination, a transformation many of us now take for granted.

Christianity essentially extended Jewish morality to non-Jews, with a few touches of its own. In antiquity, philosophy and religion operated in two completely different spheres, but Christianity merged Judaism with Greek philosophy and some of the best aspects of Roman law developing a new synthesis of its own. This synthesis built Western civilisation.

The moral sensibility found in the words of Jesus quoted above was completely unknown in the world of the Roman Empire outside of its Jewish communities.

The Christian communities made provision for their widows, who were often the most disadvantaged people in all of society. More generally, a tradition of charitable giving developed.

Slaves were permitted to become priests, something that was extremely radical at the time. And while slavery as an institution was abolished nowhere in the world for many more centuries, as Christianity influenced Roman law, the condition of slaves was improved. For example, emancipation became easier and it became illegal to separate married slaves by selling them to different masters.

Christianity was particularly attractive to women, something noted by pagan writers at the time who regarded it as a mark against the new religion.

Thanks to Christianity, Roman divorce laws were reformed so that men could not simply divorce their wives for no reason and throw them out on the streets.

The practice of exposing unwanted infants came to an end.

In addition, Christianity helped to develop in us the notion of individual responsibility by teaching us that we are all individually accountable before God for our actions, and king and peasant are judged equally and alike.

Christianity taught us that history has a direction, that it is moving towards the Kingdom of Heaven, a notion borrowed by all progressive ideologies that try to build Heaven on Earth, including, with disastrous effect, communism, which is essentially a Christian heresy.

Christianity even helped lay the foundations of modern science, contrary to popular belief. As Alfred North Whitehead, one of the great philosophers and mathematicians of the first half of the last century, explained the Middle Ages was "one long training in the intellect... in the sense of order". From this, he said, came science, which was "an unconscious derivative from medieval theology".

Even our view that the State has natural limits is derived to a large extent from Christianity which established the principle that not everything belongs to Caesar, that some things belong to God. Equally, this placed limits on the power of the Church itself.

Christianity also gave us the first universal creed, that is, a creed for everyone, hence the name of the Catholic Church, 'Catholic' meaning 'universal'.

Christianity told us to love our neighbour and by our neighbour was meant everyone. Before that, our obligations - such as they were - didn't extend beyond our families or our clan or our tribe.

All universal creeds since then, including socialism, build on the sense of universal obligation given to us by Christianity.

The welfare state, for all its present faults, arises out of this sense of obligation, and from the Christian obligation to feed the hungry, clothe the naked, to look after the sick.

In his most recent book, *Civilisation: The West and the Rest*, historian Niall Ferguson quotes a member of the Chinese Academy of Social Sciences who is adamant that the political and economic success of the West is down to Christianity.

Of course, the moral transformation begun by Christianity has not been completed and never will be, and Christians themselves have often acted in ways that were, and are, *de facto* anti-Christ.

But so profound has the influence of Christianity been on western culture, that the West would not be the West without it.

This long process of moral transformation began at the first Christmas, 2,000 years ago. As we celebrate Christmas this year, we would do well to remember our debt to Christianity. It is far greater than we think.

CHAPTER 35

TRADITIONAL FAMILY UNIT IS DYING AND WE DON'T CARE

2011

People today think they know the 'facts of life', but to judge from a new survey of attitudes to life, love and happiness, nothing could be further from the truth.

Last week Margaret Fine-Davis of Trinity College Dublin published an excellent new study called *Attitudes to Family Formation in Ireland*. It is based on a survey of 1,400 people aged 20-49.

One of its findings is that 84% of people in this age group believe it is better to live with someone before you marry them. But they are quite wrong about this.

If cohabitation is good for marriage, then how do they explain the fact that in countries where cohabitation is widespread and has been for a long time, like Sweden or Britain or America, the divorce rate is high and the marriage rate low?

In addition, 69% of respondents think cohabitation provides just as strong a basis for family life as marriage. That's not true either.

The British Millennium Cohort Study found that cohabiting parents break up twice as much as married parents.

Fifty-six percent believe that one parent can bring up a child just as well as two parents together. This can be true in individual cases, but it's not true in general.

Raising a child on your own is much harder than raising a child with another person.

To begin with, single-parent families are far more likely to be poor, and the report itself shows single mothers are the most likely to experience loneliness. This stands to reason.

How can we explain such a disparity between what people believe and what is actually true? I think it arises from a combination of wishful thinking and a reluctance to cause offence.

Because cohabitation is now so widespread, we convince ourselves that cohabitation is good for marriage.

And because we don't want to offend anyone (least of all ourselves), we say that children do just as well whether their parents are married or cohabiting or living without another adult, regardless of the evidence.

Another very good study about the family was also launched this week. Written by Tony Fahey and Peter Lunn and published by the ESRI, it examines family structure in Ireland today based on data from Census 2006.

It confirms that the Irish family is changing rapidly. The main finding is that a third of Irish families now fall outside the traditional model of a man and woman in their first marriage.

Over at The *Irish Times* the other day, Carl O'Brien – an otherwise excellent reporter – advised us all to relax about this.

He accepted that the traditional family based on marriage is the gold standard family unit, "given the positive outcomes for children in these settings".

But he then said that because this family still accounts for two-thirds of family units in Ireland, rumours of its demise are exaggerated.

On the basis of this logic, though, we should also calm down about unemployment because 85% of people are still in work, or about poverty because the vast majority of us are above the poverty line.

But no one says either of these things because an unemployment rate of 14.5% accounts for an awful lot of people in absolute terms, and likewise the poverty rate of 15.8%

In terms of the family, a quarter of children, or almost 300,000, are raised outside the marital family, which is to say outside the "gold standard family unit", as Carl O'Brien puts it. That is a lot of children.

Obviously lots of lone parents and lots of cohabiting parents do a very fine job raising their children and many do a better job than married parents.

But since the marital family is the "gold standard family unit", a figure of 300,000 should have our alarm bells ringing in the same way a 14.5% unemployment rate and a 15.8% poverty rate have our alarm bells ringing.

We should be working to strengthen and promote marriage if children are really at the heart of family policy and if we believe children ought to be raised by their own mothers and fathers.

Several factors are driving up the number of children who don't have the advantage of being raised in the "gold standard family unit".

One is separation and divorce. Another is the number of children born to lone parents. Another is cohabitation which is not the same as marriage because, as mentioned, cohabiting parents are far more likely to break up than married parents.

In fact, the number of children being raised outside of marriage in Ireland today is now high compared to a lot of other European countries, so the family in Ireland is not in rude good health, far from it.

But we remain almost entirely complacent about this. When it comes to the family, we prefer to tell ourselves comforting lies rather than face up to the facts of life.

CHAPTER 36

THERE WAS NEVER REALLY A GOLDEN AGE OF CHRISTIAN UNITY

2011

Catholics in particular like to imagine that there was a Golden Age of Christian unity that was fractured in the West by the rise of Protestantism, and five centuries before that between East and West when Constantinople and Rome split.

But for the first thousand years, they imagine, the whole of Christendom was unified, and in the West it was unified for a further 500 years.

In fact, arguably, except maybe for brief and sporadic periods, there has never really been Christian unity, properly understood. In a united Christian Church all the members would, of their own free will, agree on the essentials and disagree only on the inessentials.

But for the first 300 years or so of Christian history, no one could say there was true unity in the above sense. The heart of Christianity back then lay not in Rome and the Latin West, but in the Greek part of the Roman Empire and there were continual and sometimes violent disagreements among Christians about this or that doctrine.

When the Roman Emperor Constantine converted to Christianity, these disagreements prompted him to call the Council of Nicea in 325 AD and unity of a sort was imposed on the quarrelling Christians.

But heresies of one sort or another kept rearing their heads and the only reason some of them did not put down deep roots like Protestantism is that the ruling powers of both Church and State were able to destroy them, sometimes by force.

Had they lacked that power, Christianity would have formally split asunder much sooner than it did.

The reason East and West split in 1054 is that Rome and Constantinople were powerful enough to protect their respective Churches.

The reason Western Christianity split in 1517 is because by then there were princes both willing and able to protect the Protestant rebels.

So it was really force, not sweet reason and light that kept Christendom from formally splitting sooner than it did.

On the face of it, it seems a simple enough formula for Christians to be able to agree on the essentials and to allow disagreement on the inessentials.

Unfortunately, it seems to be part of the human condition, stemming partly from the limits of reason, that we frequently disagree over what is essential and what is inessential.

What applies to religion generally, and to Christianity, also applies to politics and philosophy. Full agreement is impossible to find and often the best we can do is not to fight – literally – over our disagreements.

After World War II, and from the Catholic point of view, after Vatican II, the current ecumenical movement developed and grew. Naively, some of its more enthusiastic proponents imagined that Christian unity was just around the corner.

But as the decades have passed we have discovered that each Christian faction (to use a slightly unfortunate word) has certain essentials they feel they cannot compromise.

For Catholics one is the Primacy of Peter. For Protestants it might be *Sola Scriptura*.

Even liberals have their doctrines. Today, liberals are dealing the biggest blows to Christian unity by insisting on women clergy, women bishops and openly homosexual clergy. They believe these things are a matter of justice, and are therefore non-negotiable.

Disagreement over these issues is tearing the Anglican Communion apart.

To the extent that liberal Anglicans forcing these things on their Communion are destroying it, and also widening the gulf between

Canterbury and Rome, not to mention between Canterbury and the Eastern Orthodox Churches.

But they believe they have no choice but to press on with their programme because, as mentioned, they believe justice demands it. That is their dogma.

All this said, however, ecumenism has been generally a great force for good. It may not have achieved the hoped-for re-union of the Churches, but it has mostly improved relations between them, and between Christians of different dominations.

On this island, for example, sectarianism in practically non-existent in the South, and is abating in the North. In the West, the main religious conflict today isn't between Christians as such, but between secularism and religion.

Secularists in particular stereotype and demonise Christians every bit as much as Catholics and Protestants once demonised each other.

Indeed, in the last century, extreme secularists have sought to exterminate religion and where that has failed, they have sought to quarantine it by restricting it purely to the private domain. The campaign to quarantine it is actually gathering strength again, including here in Ireland.

In fact, this threat to the freedom of Christians and religious believers can act to bring Christians closer together in common cause. For example, the Pope, and the present and past Archbishops of Canterbury (Rowan Williams and Lord Carey respectively), have each criticised aggressive secularism in often very similar language.

So for that matter has the Chief Rabbi of Great Britain, Jonathan Sacks.

There may never really have been a Golden Age of Christian unity, and Christian unity in the true sense may not be achievable in any case. But this does not mean Christians cannot grow closer together, humanly speaking, and it does not prevent them finding common cause where necessary. Let this be ecumenism's goal.

CHAPTER 37

AN UNEASY PEACE FOLLOWS STATE'S WAR WITH VATICAN

2011

Note: After publication of the official report dealing with abuse in Cloyne diocese, the government closed the embassy to the Holy See. The Holy See issued a response to the complaints about its behaviour during the scandals. This column was written in reaction to that.

Almost everything the public knows about both the Cloyne Report and the Vatican's response to it has been filtered through the media.

The public therefore has a very faulty understanding of both documents and where the truth lies between the Irish government and the Holy See in this whole affair.

For example, most people probably imagine that the Cloyne Report revealed that Catholic priests were sexually abusing children throughout the diocese down almost to the present day, and that the Vatican frustrated every attempt to control them.

This is simply untrue. In fact, with one exception, every concrete complaint of abuse received by the diocese post-1996 - when the Irish Church's first set of child protection guidelines were issued - related to an incident that took place before 1996, and usually long before it.

The majority of incidents took place in the 1960s and 1970s.

Therefore, even if the letter was sent to the hierarchy in 1997 giving the Vatican's take on their guidelines is as bad as its worst critics say, it made very little material difference on the ground in Cloyne.

In fact, it almost certainly made no difference because we know that the diocese's child protection officer, Monsignor Denis O'Callaghan, frequently ignored both canon law and the 1996 guidelines when dealing with allegations of child abuse.

That letter of 1997 is Exhibit A in the case against the Vatican.

And the Cloyne Report is right, it was unhelpful - although no more than that - chiefly because it had "serious reservations" about mandatory reporting.

The letter was sent by the then Papal Nuncio to the Irish bishops and it expressed the views of the Congregation for the Clergy, which was headed at the time by Cardinal Dario Castrillon Hoyos.

Among other things, Cardinal Hoyos was overly concerned about the right of accused clergy to their good name.

The proof that Cardinal Hoyos's attitude was unhelpful is the fact that in 2001, the present Pope brought about a drastic change in that mentality which has resulted in the 'defrocking' or removal from ministry of around two thousand priests worldwide.

To take the Ferns diocese as one example: since 2001, it has reported 10 priests to the civil authorities, and the same 10 to the Vatican.

Two have been convicted under civil law, and nine have been dealt with under canon law. Of the nine, six have been laicised and three have taken voluntary laicisation. One case is pending.

This proves civil law and canon law can work in parallel and complement, not compete, against one another.

(By the way, here is a pertinent question; if the critics are right, and canon law doesn't matter a damn, then why do they get upset when priests aren't 'defrocked' under canon law?)

But if that letter's reservation about mandatory reporting made life awkward for the Irish bishops, so did the Irish State because it also had serious reservations about the matter.

As the Vatican response of last weekend makes very clear, the last Fine Gael/Labour government which was in office when the 1997 letter was received by the bishops also objected to mandatory reporting.

Therefore, it is hypocritical of the current government to attack the Vatican over an attitude to mandatory reporting which it largely shared last time it was in power.

In the years since then, the Irish hierarchy has pressed successive governments to introduce mandatory reporting and it is only now that an Irish government is getting around to some version of it.

In his speech in July, Enda Kenny attacked the Vatican for frustrating "an inquiry in a sovereign democratic republic as little as three years ago".

This was treated as a virtual cause of war by the government.

Asked at the time about this incident, the government said it wasn't referring to anything specific.

Since then it has decided it was referring to the fact that the Papal Nuncio and the Vatican didn't respond to letters from the Commission of Inquiry.

But if this lack of response really did deserve such a strong attack, then the Taoiseach should also have rounded on the Office of the Minister for Children, because it was asked for information by the Commission but refused to provide it, claiming legal privilege instead.

This is extremely ironic in view of the fact that this was the same office which ordered the Cloyne inquiry in the first place. (Will the office release the required information now it has a new minister?)

So where does all this leave us? In an ideal world, the Vatican would more readily admit that the attitude of Cardinal Hoyos back in 1997 was unhelpful and the government would admit its attack was over the top, inaccurate in various ways and treated the Vatican as a virtual enemy state.

Neither has happened. But like the Vatican's response to the government, the government's response to the Vatican issued last night has avoided provocative language meaning both sides have chosen to stand down and set about rebuilding normal relations.

CHAPTER 38

THIS ATTACK ON CONFESSION IS
A THREAT TO ALL RELIGIONS

2011

Eight years ago, the US State of Maryland considered passing a law that would have required priests to break the seal of confession if the sin of child abuse was made known to them via the sacrament of Confession.

During the previous year, 2002, the Catholic Church in America had been convulsed by the child-abuse scandals in much the same way that the Church here has repeatedly been convulsed.

This set the scene for politicians in a number of states (New Hampshire and Connecticut were two others) to demand the passage of a law requiring the breaking of the seal of confession – its absolute guarantee of privacy.

Our government has embarked on a similar course, to very little opposition so far, although this may change when the relevant bill is published in the next few months and the issue comes to a head.

As in those American states, the background is the clerical-abuse scandals. But the government should note what happened in Maryland and New Hampshire and Connecticut.

In each case, the bid to attack the seal of confession was defeated, partly because of a backlash by thousands of Catholic voters, who were urged on by their bishops.

A few days ago, Cardinal Seán Brady delivered a talk in which he described the attack on the seal of confession as an attack on freedom of religion.

He said: "Freedom to participate in worship and to enjoy the long-established rites of the Church is so fundamental that any intrusion upon it is a challenge to the very basis of a free society.

"For example, the inviolability of the seal of confession is so fundamental to the very nature of the sacrament that any proposal that undermines that inviolability is a challenge to the right of every Catholic to freedom of religion and conscience."

Unlike his US counterparts, he did not ask Irish Catholics to write to their politicians in protest, but that he raised the issue at all was too much for the *Irish Times*, which attacked his remarks in a leader yesterday. It seems that Catholics are not even allowed to defend their own sacraments.

It's hard to know how many Catholics would have responded if Cardinal Brady had issued a call to arms, but if he and his fellow bishops and clergy did it often enough, clearly enough and loudly enough, then there would be a response and politicians might then have to sit up and pay attention.

However, it was not muscle power alone that caused legislators in the aforementioned American states to back down in the end; it was also because wiser heads prevailed.

For a start, the proposal is - as Seán Brady has said - an attack on religious freedom, because for Catholics, access to the sacraments is an absolutely vital and integral part of their faith.

Catholics believe that they have a divinely ordained right to confess their sins via the sacrament of Confession under an absolute assurance of privacy. They believe that the State cannot and must not interfere with this right under any circumstances.

Of course, a lot of people will dismiss this as so much mumbo jumbo. But if we can dismiss other people's most sacred beliefs and practices so contemptuously and ride roughshod over them, then religious freedom really is in peril.

There is another reason why the Government should reconsider its proposal -- a strictly practical and utilitarian one. It will do no good and may do harm because no child abuser, knowing that a priest is legally obliged to pass on his crime to the police, will go to Confession in the first place.

This is why it was completely nonsensical of the *Irish Times* in its leader yesterday to raise the case of Michael Joseph McArdle, a former Catholic priest in Australia who says he confessed child abuse on numerous occasions to numerous priests over 25 years.

Can anyone seriously believe he would have gone near a confessional if he thought that his confessor might then go to the police?

But by effectively barring a child abuser from attending Confession, the State will rob confessors of the opportunity to persuade offenders to hand themselves over to the civil authorities.

This is just one reason why the proposed law is far more likely to do harm than good.

Indeed, it is extremely doubtful whether a single crime has ever been prevented by laws requiring the breaking of the seal of confession. This partially explains why such laws are so rare around the world.

It is also why, historically speaking, laws of this sort have been found almost exclusively in extremely anti-Catholic countries, such as Britain during penal times, or in totalitarian states, which is to say, in states motivated by a wish to put Catholics in their place.

Does the Government really wish to add Ireland to that list?

Hopefully, as in New Hampshire, Maryland and Connecticut, wiser heads will prevail here in the end.

CHAPTER 39

DIDN'T I WARN YOU THAT A VOTE FOR LABOUR WAS A VOTE FOR ABORTION?

2012

Note: This column was written during the abortion debate that followed the tragic death of Savita Halappanavar in 2012.

In the run-up to the general election last year, I wrote a column that was headlined 'Any vote for the Labour party is a vote for abortion'. I was roundly attacked for this by, among other people, Michael D. Higgins.

But subsequent events have fully vindicated what I wrote at that time. Labour is pushing hard to permit abortion in Ireland on the grounds of the X Case, and members of the party including the likes of Ivana Bacik and Ciara Conway, want to go even further than this.

However, what I did not know when I cast my vote last year is that a vote for Fine Gael could soon turn out to have been a vote for abortion as well.

One reason I did not believe a vote for Fine Gael would lead to abortion in Ireland is because Fine Gael released a statement just prior to the election and the first line read simply and clearly: "Fine Gael is opposed to the legalisation of abortion."

If that is so, how can Enda Kenny possibly contemplate standing over a law that will allow abortion under the terms of the X Case?

Let's remember that the law as it stands already allows pregnancies to be ended when there is no other way to save the life of the mother.

In the case of Savita Halappanavar, we simply do not know if bringing her pregnancy to an early end was the only thing that would save her life.

But if it was, then Irish law already permits a termination in such a scenario.

Nor does this violate any kind of medical ethics. Bringing a pregnancy to an early end when that is the only way to save a pregnant woman is not considered an abortion in the moral sense of that term because it is a last resort.

The intention is not to kill the baby, and the baby will die no matter what.

However, the X Case goes beyond this. It permits a termination of pregnancy when a woman is feeling suicidal.

In this scenario it stretches credulity past breaking point to say that the only way to relieve the suicidal feeling is to kill the unborn child. For a start, it is likely that the real cause of the woman's suicidal feelings is some underlying depression and not the pregnancy itself.

Secondly, as psychiatrist Anthony McCarthy says, sometimes an abortion in such a scenario might actually make things worse, not better, for a woman.

Finally, when there are alternative means of helping a pregnant woman who is feeling suicidal other than a termination, it simply cannot be said that her baby is going to die no matter what. Both it and the mother can be saved.

Therefore, terminating a pregnancy in such a case is unethical and is an abortion in the full moral sense of that term.

This is quite apart from the fact that a law permitting abortion when a woman is feeling suicidal is wide open to abuse and will almost certainly lead over time to widespread abortion in Ireland.

When David Steel liberalised Britain's abortion law in 1967, he introduced the proviso that an abortion could only be performed on 'health' grounds if two doctors consented.

In practice, it is so easy to find two doctors to consent that roughly one pregnancy in five ends in abortion in Britain.

Steel thought this would never happen. It did. The law is completely abused. It could easily happen here too. Fine Gael and Enda Kenny also need to seriously consider the politics of this. When Fine Gael opposed the pro-life amendment of 2002, it suffered grievously in the subsequent election.

This is not the only reason or even the main reason why it suffered.

At an absolute minimum there was absolutely no electoral dividend for opposing that amendment, and all the Fine Gael TDs who were most actively against it lost their seats, including Alan Shatter.

Following the Shatter line on this will have deadly consequences for many Fine Gael TDs at the next election. Pro-life voters – and there are still plenty of them – will not forget it if Fine Gael permits Labour to introduce abortion to Ireland, as distinct from genuinely life-saving treatment, which is already available here.

If Fine Gael does pave the way for abortion, the only proper response from pro-life Fine Gael voters will be to vote only for those Fine Gael TDs who are clearly pro-life and who are willing to lose the party whip if and when this goes to the vote.

Enda Kenny has a fateful decision to make. If he simply codifies existing practice he will meet little or no opposition.

But if he goes further than that, he will be remembered as the Taoiseach who introduced the direct killing of unborn children to Ireland only weeks after the passage of the Children Rights Referendum.

Is this really how he wants to be remembered?

CHAPTER 40

MEDIA RUSHES TO JUDGE BUT WE DON'T KNOW FACTS

2012

Note: This story was written just as news of the death of Savita Halappanavar broke. Her death while miscarrying sparked another abortion debate.

The British media, in tandem with the Irish, is running with the 'woman dies because she was denied abortion' story headline.

It's not surprising that the likes of *The Guardian* would give the story prominence because *The Guardian* is fiercely pro-abortion.

In Britain it fits in with a certain stereotype of this country to believe that women are dying here because of our lingering adherence to Catholic medical ethics.

However, even the more pro-life *Daily Telegraph* and *Daily Mail* have given the story prominence. That would be justified if we knew that Savita Halappanavar did indeed die specifically because she was denied an abortion, but that is not why she died.

We know this because if there was a need to end her pregnancy in order to save her life, then the hospital was free to do that. Nothing in law was preventing the hospital from doing so.

And to be absolutely clear, ending a woman's pregnancy prematurely is not necessarily the same thing as abortion.

For example, inducing labour where it is necessary to save the life of the mother is not the same as abortion and Irish hospitals induce labour in these circumstances on a regular basis.

From the available facts, we know that Mrs Halappanavar was miscarrying and that she died within days of being admitted to hospital from septicaemia and E Coli ESBL.

We do not know for certain whether ending the pregnancy upon her arrival in the hospital would have saved her life, but to repeat, if medical staff needed to do that they could have done it.

Therefore the 'woman dies because she was denied abortion' storyline is simply not true. The 'woman dies because of Catholic opposition to abortion' is also not true.

We simply do not know for certain at this stage whether Mrs Halappanavar would have died no matter what was done. This is what the investigation into her death will ascertain.

And we must also repeat for the umpteenth time that Ireland has one of the lowest maternal death rates in the world. It is lower than the British rate where abortion is available on demand.

In addition, it is necessary to remind ourselves that sometimes women die because of botched abortions in legal settings. Indeed, last year a doctor – Phanuel Dartey – was struck off in Britain because he nearly killed an Irish woman while performing an abortion on her in a Marie Stopes Clinic in the UK.

This story received remarkably little publicity here in Ireland. RTÉ did not cover it at all, whereas it has given the Savita Halappanavar story wall-to-wall coverage. Why this discrepancy?

And by what journalistic calculus did RTÉ decide to give so little coverage to the revelation that some staff at pregnancy crisis agencies in Ireland are giving women dangerous and illegal advice? It would be good to know.

There has been a tremendous and unseemly rush to judgment in this case.

It is being used to advance the argument that Ireland must change its law on abortion before we know the full facts.

It is also being used to falsely and unjustly give the impression that Ireland is an unsafe place for pregnant women when the opposite is true.

The bottom line is that we cannot draw any decisive conclusions about what happened in this tragic case until we do know all the facts.

CHAPTER 41

ENDA CAN WIELD THE STICK
BUT CHURCH TAKES A HIDING

2013

Again and again, I contrast in my mind the praise Enda Kenny has received in many quarters for his ruthless treatment of his party colleagues who voted against the new abortion law, and the condemnation the Vatican has received for its much milder treatment of dissident priests such as Fr Tony Flannery.

The Vatican made a very big mistake taking disciplinary action against Fr Flannery. In doing so it gave him a platform and an enhanced moral status. He is now seen as a martyr for his beliefs.

On the strength of it, he has a new book out called A Question of Conscience. He has been interviewed many times on radio, usually in the most unchallenging and sympathetic way, and only the other day Fr Iggy O'Donovan, another priest not well got in the Vatican, defended him publicly, receiving sympathetic coverage of his own into the bargain.

It is a rare thing indeed for priests such as Fr Iggy and Fr Flannery to be asked tough questions or to have to debate with a critic in the presence of a neutral presenter.

On Monday on RTÉ radio, Sean O'Rourke did gently probe Fr Iggy and managed to get him to concede that priests can and should be held account-able by Church authorities. But when asked to name something that is being done today in the name of Christianity that will be seen by future ages, and by the Church itself, as a 'perversion', he didn't really come up with anything.

The sex scandals don't come into this category because, unlike, say, the Crusades, they were not done in the name of Christianity.

As for Fr Flannery, I can't remember a single interview in which he has been asked any truly challenging question.

On the question of the nature of the Eucharist, for example, his views appear indistinguishable from those of many Protestants. Is it so hard for an interviewer to ask him, point-blank, whether he believes that at the moment of consecration the bread and wine become the actual body and blood of Christ?

And is it so hard for an interviewer to ask him whether or not he accepts that the Church, just like any other organisation, has a right to impose disciplinary procedures on its members in certain circumstances?

Perhaps Lucinda Creighton and her fellow expelled TDs and senators should also publish a book and also call it 'A Question of Conscience'. They paid a much heavier price than Fr Flannery for their actions. They have been expelled, which is to say, excommunicated from their parliamentary party.

Maybe this is one reason why Micheál Martin accused Enda Kenny of echoing Charlie Haughey's "uno duce, una voce", Mussolini-esque style of leadership

Very few radio panellists that I have heard, and very few commentators generally, have said that the 'Fine Gael Seven' should not have been expelled. The more general line is that Enda Kenny has proved his toughness, and his action was the only way to maintain party discipline.

Furthermore, it has been said that it will be difficult for him to allow them back into the parliamentary party because that would tell the rest of the Fine Gael TDs and senators that there is no real punishment for breaking the whip, and no real reward for obeying the whip, when they were under considerable public pressure to do otherwise during the abortion debate.

But if it is okay for Fine Gael to take strong action to maintain discipline and the coherence of party policy, then why is it not okay for the Church to do so?

Here is the explanation for the contradiction: those praising Kenny and attacking the Vatican simply want to have their way, by whatever means.

They wanted abortion legislated for under the terms of the X case, and they want the Catholic Church to change its teaching in line with their wishes.

Therefore, they supported the disciplining of Lucinda Creighton, Terence Flanagan, Brian Walsh, Fidelma Healy Eames, Billy Timmins, Peter Mathews and Paul Bradford and oppose the disciplining of Fr Tony Flannery *et al.*

So it's not the use of discipline per se that they oppose. They like it when it suits them, and they oppose it when it suits them. That is to say, they are entirely hypocritical about the matter. And they get away with it and probably can't even see the contradiction half the time.

There is, however, a big difference between the Fine Gael Seven and Fr Tony Flannery that ought to be pointed out, namely this: when Lucinda *et al* joined Fine Gael they never thought they would be asked to vote for abortion. Their party shifted ground, they did not.

BUT when Fr Tony Flannery became a priest he knew exactly what the Church stood for. He now doubts many of the teachings of his Church and he expects the Church to accommodate him.

It is also very notable that Fr Flannery, who is presenting himself as a hero of conscience, said not one word in support of the Fine Gael Seven when they were punished for standing up for their beliefs.

Nor did he utter one word in opposition to the new abortion law, not even those parts that directly attack conscience rights and would force Catholic hospitals to perform abortions under the terms of the law.

If Fr Flannery really believed in conscience rights, he would have spoken out against the expulsion of the Fine Gael rebels at an absolute minimum. His silence was very telling. Would an interviewer care to put that to him one day?

CHAPTER 42

A PROPORTIONATE VIEW OF THE MAGDALENE LAUNDRIES

2013

Note: Martin McAleese was appointed by the government to investigate what took place in the Magdalene laundries. This column was written in response to the publication of that report.

Last Friday night's *God Slot* on RTÉ radio broadcast an interview with two nuns who had worked in Magdalene homes.

This was the first interview of its kind and the nuns granted it on condition of anonymity because they were scared of the backlash that would follow if their names became public.

The nuns had four main points. The first was that Ireland during the era of the Magdalene homes was extremely poor and this must be taken into account when assessing the place of the laundries in Irish society.

The second was that women who fell outside society's norms were more harshly treated than men.

The third was that women ended up in the Magdalene homes for a variety of reasons, and the fourth was that the homes have been judged by a very anti-Catholic media.

So, how poor was Ireland in the middle part of the last century? By one calculation based on CSO data, in real terms Ireland in 1935 was less than a tenth as rich then as it is today, even taking into account the present recession.

The following figures give us a further insight. In 1946, there were 662,654 households in Ireland. Almost half of these had no indoor toilet and no outdoor toilet. That is, they still relied on bedpans and the like as people had done for centuries before.

To put it another way, in the middle of the last century, the living conditions of many Irish people were not so different from those of their distant ancestors.

Life expectancy was also much lower. In 1926, the life expectancy for males and females was 57.4 and 57.9 years respectively. Today it is 76.8 and 81.6 years respectively.

The much lower life expectancy meant that many children lost one or both parents. In 1946, 13.8% of children aged 14 had lost one parent, most commonly the mother, and 1.1% had lost both parents.

There was no welfare state in those years and the answer to many of the problems created by grinding poverty was institutionalisation.

This is clear from the Martin McAleese investigation into the Magdalene homes. The two nuns on the *God Slot* were quite correct to imply that if these places did not exist, many of their inmates would have been on the street instead.

They could have added that they might have been in prison instead (in a small minority of cases) or remained with abusive parents or been placed in mental institutions. (Which may or may not have been better than the Magdalene laundries).

In a sense, we need to consider two separate issues when examining the Magdalene homes and their legacy. The first is the justification for institutions in themselves and the second is what actually took place inside them.

Without question, institutions in general were justified in their day. In conditions of great poverty when there simply wasn't the money available to alleviate many of the problems caused by poverty (including the early death of parents), what alternative was there?

And if the institutions had not been run by the religious orders, someone would have had to run them. This would likely have meant fewer institutions and it is highly unlikely they would have been run any better than the orders ran them to judge from the record of lay-run institutions both here and overseas.

Today, foster care is often the alternative to institutional case but foster parents are paid over €1,200 per month per foster child. If that money weren't available, there would still be thousands of children in institutions.

As for the Magdalene homes themselves, how bad were they? They certainly were not as bad as portrayed in the film, *The Magdalene Sisters*, or in some of the popular accounts generally.

For example, they were not set up for single mothers and few of their residents/inmates were single mothers. Indeed, those who spent time in them were rarely in for 'sexual sins' at all.

Second, the average length of stay was seven months, and not years as many people still seem to think.

Third, sexual and physical abuses were very rare.

Fourth, they were not money-making enterprises and for the most part barely broke even.

Fifth, the average age of the women who were placed in them was 23 and finally, in all about 10,000 passed through their doors over a 70-year period and not 30,000 as previously believed.

All of this is clear from the Martin McAleese's inquiry into the laundries but in many ways, he might as well not have written the report at all because very quickly, the movie version of the Magdalene homes was reinstalled in the public mind, namely that they were highly abusive places in which women were placed because of sexual sins.

For example, at one point in his second address to the Dáil on the matter, Enda Kenny says women were placed in them for being out of step with the "sort of moral code that was fostered at the time".

But the McAleese Report makes clear that this is not why they were placed in them in the vast majority of cases, something the Taoiseach points out later on in his speech contradicting what he said at an earlier point in the same speech.

One hundred and eighteen women testified to the McAleese investigation about their time in the laundries. Some commentators have suggested that their evidence was not representative of most of the women who passed through them.

But 53 of the 118 women who testified were from the Magdalene campaigning groups so was their account also unrepresentative?

Indeed, if the account of the 118 is unrepresentative, including that of the 53, then by this logic we cannot ever know what really happened in these institutions and should therefore be silent about it.

What, therefore, can we say about them? I think we can say that they were not Ireland's version of Stalin's gulag as some insist on saying.

I think we can say they were badly misnamed because their name gave the impression that the women in them were 'fallen' even though they were not.

I think we can also say, in agreement with Martin McAleese, that they were harsh and cold places for much of their history and often fell far below the standards we should expect of places that are properly Christian.

If we could wind back the clock, what would we do differently? Given the poverty of the time and the lack of alternatives, we would still have had versions of the Magdalene homes, but they would not have been called that and they would have been more humanely run.

In the end, the best advice for anyone interested in this topic is simply to read the McAleese Report for themselves, and at the very least the introduction by Mr McAleese.

This will provide you with a more accurate account of these institutions than media reports determined to perpetuate an image of the Magdalene homes that is frequently at variance with the facts.

CHAPTER 43

A PROTESTANT TAOISEACH WOULD NOT DO THE THINGS KENNY HAS

2013

Would the Catholic Church be better off if we had a Protestant as Taoiseach rather than Enda Kenny? I ask the question because Enda seems to go to such great lengths to show he is not a stooge of his own church.

The question is further prompted by something he said in the Dáil on Wednesday in response to Mattie McGrath.

Mattie asked him if he understood why some people simply could not accept that the Abortion Bill is pro-life even though Mr Kenny insists that it is.

Enda responded by referring to the abusive messages he has received from some people opposed to the Bill including one that said he is a 'murderer'. (I've been told I should be "castrated and hung up on O'Connell Street", and that I "should have been aborted", among many other choice threats and insults.)

But then Mr Kenny said that while he is a Taoiseach who happens to be a Catholic, he is not a Catholic Taoiseach.

Why did he feel the need to say this? Would Ruairi Quinn who was sitting right beside him ever tell the Dáil, "I'm a Taoiseach who happens to be a Social Democrat, but I'm not a Social Democrat Taoiseach?" The idea is ridiculous.

Ruairi Quinn is in politics because he is a Social Democrat and because he wants Ireland to be Social Democratic. Enda Kenny will claim that he can't be a Catholic Taoiseach because not everyone in Ireland is a Catholic. Absolutely true. But not everyone is a Social Democrat either. In fact, there are far fewer Social Democrats than there are practicing Catholics.

I'm not a Social Democrat. I don't think Social Democracy would be good for Ireland, but if Ruairi Quinn had his way I'd end up living in a Social Democratic Ireland regardless. Fine Gael used to be a Christian Democrat party. Could you imagine a European politician ever saying, 'I'm a politician who happens to be a Christian Democrat, but I'm not a Christian Democrat politician'? Never.

Christians established Christian Democratic parties all over Western Europe after the war with the express intention of getting into power and implementing their Christian Democrat policies. They were very success-ful for a long time.

Does Enda Kenny think those parties were somehow suspect from a democratic point of view?

Those parties were, among other things, pro-life. They were pro-life partly because many members of those parties were Catholic. But they weren't protecting the right to life of the unborn simply because that was the 'Catholic' thing to do. They did it because they believed it was the right thing to do, period.

Enda Kenny seems to think that if he removes the suicide clause from the Abortion Bill then he will be legislating only for Catholics.

However, if he removed the suicide clause he wouldn't be legislating only for Catholics, he would simply be protecting the right to life of the unborn.

Mr Kenny may have convinced himself that this really is a 'pro-life' Bill but the fact is that it will allow the deliberate and intentional destruction of unborn human lives when a woman is deemed to be suicidal even though there will always be alternatives to abortion available. If the Bill really is pro-life then he needs to ask himself why not a single pro-life group sup-ports it and why the likes of Ivana Bacik see it as a first step.

He also needs to ask himself why up to 40,000 people took to the streets in Dublin last weekend to protest against the Bill if it really is pro-life? That was the biggest demonstration of the year of any sort and the pro-life cam-paign organised it in just three weeks.

As I say, Enda seems to feel the need to prove time and again that he does not 'defer' to the Catholic Church, that in this respect at least, he is his own man.

He 'proved' it with his thundering denunciation of the Vatican two years ago. He did it again when he allowed our embassy to the Holy See to be closed.

He did it when he permitted the passage of a law that requires the breaking of the Seal of Confession, making us one of the only countries in the world with such a law.

He did it when he was using his mobile phone in front of Pope Benedict, something he would not have done in front of the Queen.

He is doing it now in allowing the Abortion Bill to ride roughshod over the consciences of pro-life doctors and the ethos of pro-life hospitals (making us more extreme than the UK in this respect).

And of course he is doing it most of all by permitting abortion when a woman is deemed to be suicidal, despite the fact that there is no evidence a single woman will thereby be saved.

Would a Protestant Taoiseach – or rather a Taoiseach who happened to be Protestant – do all these things?

I can't imagine it. I can't imagine a Protestant Taoiseach closing the embassy to the Holy See or playing with his mobile phone in front of the Pope, or requiring doctors to go against their deepest conscientious beliefs.

Enda needs to know we get it. We know he's not the stooge of the Catholic Church. He has proven it abundantly. From here on in, therefore, he should just do the right thing, even if that happens to be the Catholic thing also.

CHAPTER 44

IF THERE IS NO GOD, NO LAW-GIVER, THEN WHY SHOULD WE BE EQUAL?

2013

Let us first of all remind ourselves that Martin Luther King was a Baptist pastor. Any account of him which leaves out or diminishes that fact does a terrible disservice to the man because the inspiration for his civil rights campaign came first and foremost from his deep Christian faith.

This week is the 50th anniversary of his magnificent, 'I have a dream' speech delivered in Washington DC in front of the Lincoln Memorial, another man who cannot be understood properly without understanding his Christian faith.

Read King's speech, listen to his speech, and what you encounter is a religious sermon delivered almost from top to bottom delivered in the mesmeric cadences of the black southern preacher, which is what King was, just like his father before him.

In his speech he tells us that "all men are created equal", that is, created by a creator, which is to say, God.

He tells the crowd that we must "make justice a reality for all of God's children". He talks about the redemptive power of 'unearned suffering', a deeply Christian idea.

He ends with the words of the old Negro spiritual (his description): "Free at last! Free at last! Thank God Almighty, we are free at last!"

King was fighting the lasting effects of racism and slavery in America, both of which found a theological and a 'scientific' justification.

Christian racists in effect rejected the doctrine that all men are created equal. They believed that God intended some races to be servant races.

Racism also derived plenty of support from the 'scientific' doctrine of Social Darwinism and the idea that the white man had won the battle to be the 'fittest'.

It took World War II to destroy the respectability of Social Darwinism and its close cousin, eugenics.

Stemming from his belief in God, King also believed in a moral law that was higher than any lawman could make.

He made this abundantly clear in his *Letter from Birmingham Jail* when his critics were asking him, "how can you justify obeying some laws and disobeying others?" He was in prison for civil disobedience.

He answered: "I would be the first to advocate obeying just laws. One has not only a legal but also a moral responsibility to obey just laws. Conversely, one has a moral responsibility to disobey unjust laws. I would agree with St Augustine that 'an unjust law is no law at all'."

Then he added the punch line: "Now, what is the difference between the two? How does one determine whether a law is just or unjust? A just law is a man-made code that squares with the moral law or the law of God. An unjust law is a code that is out of harmony with the moral law. To put it in the terms of St Thomas Aquinas: An unjust law is a human law that is not rooted in eternal law and natural law."

Not alone is there hardly a politician in Ireland who would come out with a sentence like that today, there are few enough priests or bishops either, of any Church. They know they would stand accused of 'fundamentalism'.

But if there is no God, then what law can possibly be higher than man-made law? If there is no law-giver above us, then we are the only law-givers.

This notion that the only law is the law of the land led the ostensibly Catholic St Vincent's hospital to say recently that it would implement the new abortion law because it always follows the law.

In other words, for St Vincent's hospital there is no law higher than civil law. Martin Luther King would profoundly disagree with that. As would Abraham Lincoln.

When King said "all men are created equal", he was quoting the American Declaration of Independence, itself effectively a theological as well as a political statement.

But if civil law decides we are not equal and there is no higher law we can appeal to, how can we say it is 'unjust'?

King would say, we can't.

In fact, if there is no God, and we are simply a by-product of blind evolution, then why should we be equal? By what principle do we arrive at such a notion other than that it suits us to believe in it?

Politics is full of human rights talk. However, this presupposes there is some kind of a moral law, higher than the civil law, which the civil law must conform to.

Again, Luther would say there is no higher moral law if there is no God, no ultimate law-giver, no creator of our rights, our 'inalienable' rights as Bunreacht Na hEireann puts it. There are simply the 'rights' that the State chooses to give us.

Martin Luther King's 'dream' speech is rightly celebrated as a great civil rights speech.

But it stems from a deep theological and philosophical vision, one that depends on believing in a creator God and in a moral and natural law which he gave us and against which our laws much be judged.

CHAPTER 45

WHEN BOKO HARAM WAS 'MERELY' KILLING CHRISTIANS THE WORLD LOOKED AWAY

2014

In mid-February the Nigerian terrorist group Boko Haram, currently making headlines around the world, attacked the Christian village of Izghe in the north of the country killing at least 106 people and specifically targeting male residents.

This attack, one of many on Christians by Boko Haram, attracted almost no international publicity, much less celebrities posting pictures of themselves online condemning the attack.

What has finally made Boko Haram almost a household name in the West is their kidnapping of over 200 mainly Christian schoolgirls for the 'crime' of receiving a Western education.

Boko Haram is actually the nickname of the organisation. It means 'Western education is forbidden'. The full Arabic version of their name means 'People Committed to the Propagation of the Prophet's Teachings and Jihad'.

They take their inspiration from a text in the Koran which says, "Anyone who is not governed by what Allah has revealed is among the transgressors".

They were founded in 2002 as an ultra-Islamic group and since 2009 have been attempting to found an Islamic state through violence. Their violence has frequently targeted Christians but also Muslims opposed to them.

They are against anyone, male or female, receiving a 'Western' education, or indeed coming under any kind of 'Western' influence.

They associate Western education with Christian education and there is a good reason for this because Christian missionaries, mainly Irish Holy Ghost Fathers set up schools all over southern Nigeria for both boys and girls.

A Holy Ghost Father (or 'Spiritan' as they're now called) told me the other day that there was big resistance in the Muslim north of the country to them setting up schools there, even though there is a (now rapidly diminishing) Christian population in the north.

Some of the more obtuse critics of religion think religion is all of the same kind, all equally bad and that what is done in the name of one religion reflects on all religions. But that is like claiming politics is all of the same kind and crimes committed in the name of one form of politics is a stain on all kinds of politics.

It is obvious that we should distinguish between bad and good politics and bad and good religion. Terrible things have been done in the name of Christianity but today Christianity is overwhelmingly peaceful in all parts of the world. Instead, most religious violence is carried out in the name of Islam which is in a militant phase. Violent Muslim groups tend to be called 'Islamist' and so Boko Haram is often called 'Islamist'.

This Islamist group would obviously be violently opposed to everything Irish missionaries have done in Nigeria over the last hundred years and will literally stop at nothing to stop Christian influence spreading to the north of the country. That are killing Christians to force Christians to move to the south of the country and they are succeeding.

The question arises, why hasn't the world cared about this? Why did it take the kidnapping of those schoolgirls to make us start paying attention? There are two reasons in all probability. One is that the Western world hasn't shown much concern for what is happening to Christians in other parts of the world for decades.

This is because we are much more secular than we were and all because many of us are now very hostile towards Christianity. It is all because it is very hard for us in the once Christian-dominated West to imagine that Christians can be a persecuted minority anywhere even though Christianity is now the most persecuted religion in the world with thousands if not tens of thousands of Christians being killed each year because of their faith.

This is causing Christians to abandon parts of the world where they have lived since the dawn of Christianity. Christians in much of the Middle East are extremely beleaguered and there is almost no fuss in the West about it. That is a scandal. Not even Western Christians seem to care much and that is an even greater scandal.

A second reason for the sudden interest in the activities of Boko Haram is the fact that they targeted girls on this occasion. Education is obviously one of the best ways to empower any group and an attack on the education of girls is an attack on female empowerment. Therefore the attack on these girls is an attack on the ideals of feminism, although not only feminism seeing as so many schools in Nigeria, as elsewhere in the world, were founded by Christians.

But the fact is that feminism is far more fashionable cause in the West than Christianity and this explains why this latest incident has caused so many headlines compared with the killing and shooting of Christians.

It is why Michelle Obama had a photograph posted of herself online calling for the girls to be freed and it why so many celebrities have jumped on the bandwagon.

It also explains why the feminist protest group in Russia, Pussy Riot, became a *cause célèbre* in the West after they were arrested and served time in prison for staging a protest in Moscow's Cathedral of Christ the Saviour.

In Russia, Christian groups not approved by the state, often American Evangelicals, are attacked, harassed and arrested. This attracts no international attention to speak of much less interviews on top rating shows in the West, much less on RTÉ.

So it is a good thing indeed that Boko Haram is finally attracting the international attention and condemnation it deserves but it should have attracted this attention years ago but didn't because the persecution of Christians is simply not a fashionable cause in the West.

CHAPTER 46

THE CHURCH'S VITAL ROLE IN THE FALL OF THE BERLIN WALL

2014

Events to mark the 25th anniversary of the fall of the Berlin Wall took place in Germany at the weekend. The 'fall of the wall' was a truly momentous moment in European history. More than anything else the Berlin Wall symbolised a divided continent.

The Berlin Wall was also an enormous, daily reminder of the failure of communism to fulfil its promises. It was built not to keep people out, but to keep people in. It was built to stop East Germans fleeing into West Berlin to live in the capitalist West.

But why would people want to flee the 'workers' paradise'? Surely it should have been the other way around? Surely people should have been flocking into the workers' paradise if that is indeed what it was? It wasn't of course. It was anything but.

People in the West are still not familiar enough with the reality of life under communism. For some reason, film-makers have almost never gone near the subject.

There was a time when Christians were aware of just how bad life could be for their fellow Christians behind the Iron Curtain, but that has also faded.

In the USSR, Lenin and Stalin attempted to stamp out religion completely. The methods used in Eastern Europe following the communist take-over were slightly more subtle and varied, although the aim was the same; exterminate religion.

In Hungary there was a massive confrontation between the Catholic Church and the new Communist Government. Cardinal Josef Mindszenty refused point blank to cooperate with the Government and thereby to lend it any legitimacy.

As Anne Applebaum writes in her book *Iron Curtain: The Crushing of Eastern Europe*: "Church schools and institutions had been destroyed, innocent people had been arrested and killed, and he had the courage to say so".

For his troubles, he was imprisoned and tortured by the communists and then spent years in the American embassy in Budapest waiting for permission to leave the country after his position in Hungary became hopeless.

In Poland, Cardinal Stefan Wyszynski adopted a different approach. First of all, the Catholic Church in Poland was more powerful than it was in Hungary and the authorities were a bit more reluctant to try and crush it. Secondly, Wyszynski was less confrontational by nature than Mindszenty.

He signed a Church-state agreement and his sermons about the situation of the Church were soft-spoken. Applebaum writes that this "left ordinary people feeling confused about the Church's real attitude to communism".

However, this didn't stop the communists eventually arresting Wyszynski although he was never put on trial.

Poland's communist government also went to great lengths to try and co-opt Polish priests. For example, it recruited 'progressive priests' who admired communism. They became known as 'patriotic priests'.

At one point the number of such priests had grown to 1,000, but they met strong resistance from the hierarchy and from ordinary Catholics.

In any case, as admirable as Mindszenty was, Wyszynski's approach might have been the wiser because the Catholic Church in Poland emerged from the hyper-aggressive Stalinist era in much better shape than its Hungarian counterpart and this, of course, helped to pave the way for the eventual downfall of European communism and the Berlin Wall.

A key event in the run-up to the fall of European communism was the election of St John Paul II as Pope in 1978. John Paul cast aside the foreign policy of the Holy See which in the previous decade or so has decided that the best approach to European communism was one of conciliation.

Wyszynski's approach seems to show that some level of conciliation with communism could work in the right circumstances. But by the same token, a more direct, confrontational approach is also called for in the right circumstances.

St John Paul made it abundantly clear that he believed communism was a failed and broken system and could never be anything except that.

St John Paul always believed – rightly – that unless you got your view of Man right, you would get nothing right. He saw that communism saw Man as essentially a material being and excluded God entirely from the picture. (He also saw, by the way, that capitalism did the same thing but at the same time that capitalism never built gulags, unlike communism).

As a Pole, it was impossible for the Poland's communist Government to refuse John Paul's wish to visit his native country soon after his election as Pontiff.

When he did so, millions turned out for him in a massive expression not just of faith, but of national identity. Poles wished to be free of communism.

When the Solidarity movement emerged in Poland, led by Lech Walesa, it received huge moral support from St John Paul.

Even though the Polish Government imposed martial law in an attempt to retain control of the country, it could not resist the popular will, especially not now that the Soviet Union was unwilling to use its army to violently suppress Solidarity and its supporters.

John Paul alone cannot, of course, be credited alone with the fall of European communism and the Berlin Wall, but he played a major part, something acknowledged by the Soviet leader at the time the Wall fell, namely Mikhail Gorbachev.

Would communism have fallen so soon if the Church had been weaker? Probably not. Because the Church in Poland remained strong, it meant that the state could never become as powerful as it wanted to be and therefore could not seize complete control over the minds of the people which is what all totalitarian states want.

Had the Catholics of Poland decided to abandon the Church, or else to become 'spiritual' as distinct from religious (by 'spiritual' in this context I mean a highly individualised faith that detaches itself from authority and has only a semi-detached relationship with the faith community), life would have been made much easier for the communist Government.

But because the Church held open a space in the public square that the state could not control, that space become a focal point of resistance to the state's totalist claims.

St John Paul II then took advantage of that. Any explanation of the fall of the Berlin Wall that leaves out the vital role the Church played in that, is simply wilfully ignorant.

CHAPTER 47

SINGLE MOTHERS WERE CRUELLY TREATED THE WORLD OVER

2014

*Note: This column was written in response to the furore
that surrounded the revelation that 800 infants died at
Tuam's mother and baby home.*

When the inquiry into the Magdalene homes was announced a couple of years ago, I wrote a column challenging three myths about them. The first is that they were an Irish phenomenon only. They were not.

The second is that they were Catholic only. They were not. The third is that they were chiefly for unmarried mothers. They were not. The subsequent McAleese Report backed all of this up.

With respect to our mother and baby homes, similar myths are taking hold, chiefly that they were a particularly Irish and particularly Catholic phenomenon. They were not.

In particular, what has taken root is the notion that Ireland, once the most Catholic country in Western Europe, was also a waking nightmare, chiefly because of the Church's teachings on human sexuality.

It is true that Irish Catholicism was once in the grip of a spirituality that laid for too much emphasis on sin and punishment but it is not true to say that what we did to single mothers was uniquely Irish or uniquely Catholic.

Single mothers were treated appallingly almost everywhere.

For example, Britain had mother and child homes from the 1890s until the 1960s. The first ones were established by the Salvation Army.

The website motherandbabyhomes.com describes well the philosophy behind them. It says: "Premarital pregnancy was heavily stigmatised and provoked issues around sex, morality, religion and authority both parental and community. While there were women who birthed and raised their il-legitimate children, there were many who were feared (sic) to have brought shame upon the family and quickly ushered into the confines of a Mother and Baby Home to hide their pregnancies. Often orchestrated by social work-ers, or parents of the young woman, many were pressured into giving their children up for adoption with an all-time peak in 1968 of adoption orders granted in England, 16,164 in all."

Every bit of that should be very familiar to us and it alone shows that our attitude to single mothers was not uniquely or even particularly Irish or Catholic.

But perhaps we can expect to find a better attitude elsewhere. What about the Swedish welfare paradise? Surely there, single mothers and their children were treated in an enlightened manner?

In Sweden the 'solution' was sometimes to sterilise unmarried mothers. They also made some have abortions. They also had institutions in which abuse was widespread. The policy of sterilising unmarried mothers was explicitly a Social Democratic policy and lasted from the mid-1930s until the mid-1970s.

It was a form of eugenics. The mentally handicapped were sterilised and so were tens of thousands considered to be guilty of 'asocial' behaviour. That category included unmarried mothers.

'Asocial' types were considered to be a threat to a well-functioning welfare state. They were offered financial inducements to be sterilised, but victims of the policy have testified that they were sometimes forcibly ster-ilised and made to have abortions.

Try to imagine these stories on the Irish airwaves. Try to imagine women describing how the Irish State had sterilised them so that they could have no more children, even after they married, and in some cases had aborted the only child they would ever have.

Now try to make the story stick that our treatment of unmarried moth-ers was somehow particularly Irish and particularly Catholic.

Ask yourself also why so few people know that tens of thousands of Swedes (95% of them women) were sterilised as a result of a policy designed to eliminate 'asocial' behaviour. Ask yourself why the international media hasn't given this the same obsessive and hysterical coverage it has given to the Tuam babies story, one that has been exaggerated in many cases out of all proportion?

When a given country and a given religion are constantly singled out and their sins held up before the world in this way, we have a right to ask why this is so.

Why is it so? Other countries have had terrible scandals. Other countries treated unmarried mothers and their children appallingly. Other religions had the same attitude to unmarried mothers, and very secular, social democratic countries like Sweden were ruthless towards them.

Why does it suit so many people, here and overseas, to paint Catholic Ireland as a dystopia, something on a par with Stalin's Russia or Pol Pot's Cambodia and why are our politicians, including Enda Kenny, so inclined to go along with this?

What is also incredible is that some of the same people who are waxing most indignant about the mother and child homes think an equivalent scandal today is the fact that 4,000 Irish women have to travel to England each year for abortions. But that is how we deal with unwanted children today; we abort them, and many of us want them to be aborted on Irish soil in the name of 'choice'. There are no graves, marked or unmarked for these children. So we should not be proud of how we deal with unwanted children today and we should not be proud of the fact that we often prefer abortion to adoption. We are to have the inevitable and necessary inquiry into the homes. But it cannot simply focus on Church-run mother-and-baby homes. It must also look at the county homes. In addition, it must look at how other countries dealt with unmarried mothers and their children for the sake of fairness.

That is to say, the inquiry must be properly rounded, not driven by an agenda, and give us real insights into how we should deal today with 'inconvenient' children.

CHAPTER 48

HOW THE WORLD'S MEDIA
MISREPORTED THE TUAM STORY

2014

There is a willingness to believe the worst about Catholic Ireland.

I was at a conference a few days ago and a delegate from Chile came up to me and asked out of genuine curiosity what the nuns did to the babies in Tuam. A delegate from Croatia asked me the same thing. They are both practising Catholics and were doubtful about the story but the fact that someone from Chile and someone else from Croatia asked me about the Tuam babies story showed how widely it has been reported.

What the two people had picked up, of course, were the reports that the nuns had 'dumped' the bodies of almost 800 babies in a septic tank. *The Irish Examiner*, in possibly the most exaggerated comment on the whole episode, described it, and other stories that have emerged from our institutions, as 'Ireland's holocaust'.

Even the *Washington Post* and the *Boston Globe* were taken in by the original, horror movie version of the story. The former ran with the headline, "800 skeletons of babies found inside tank at former Irish home for unwed mothers", while the later said, "Galway historian finds 800 babies in septic tank grave".

The Associated Press, upon which many media outlets all over the world rely on for their international coverage, ended up having to clarify various important aspects of its coverage.

But it only did this after being challenged by *America* magazine, a Jesuit publication.

Having been challenged by *America,* AP responded:

"In stories published June 3 and June 8 about young children buried in unmarked graves after dying at a former Irish orphanage for the children of unwed mothers, the Associated Press incorrectly reported that the children had not received Roman Catholic baptisms; documents show that many children at the orphanage were baptised.

"The AP also incorrectly reported that Catholic teaching at the time was to deny baptism and Christian burial to the children of unwed mothers; although that may have occurred in practice at times it was not Church teaching.

"In addition, in the June 3 story, the AP quoted a researcher who said she believed that most of the remains of children who died there were interred in a disused septic tank; the researcher has since clarified that without excavation and forensic analysis it is impossible to know how many sets of remains the tank contains, if any.

"The June 3 story also contained an incorrect reference to the year that the orphanage opened; it was 1925, not 1926."

That last little bit about the date is only a detail. The rest is not. It is not a 'detail' to report that the children were unbaptised. In fact, the only children the Church will not baptise are those who are stillborn because the Church does not baptise the dead for obvious reasons.

If the nuns running the Tuam mother and baby home were not allowing the children to be baptised that would have been completely against Church teaching. But as the AP now admits, the records show "many of the children were baptised". If some were not baptised it is almost certain it is because they died before it could happen.

The original AP story made things worse by saying it was actually against Church teaching to baptise the children of unmarried mothers. They could easily have checked this out and found it to be completely untrue. Why didn't they?

Finally, AP, like many other media outlets, was very quick to believe that the nuns had dumped the bodies of the babies in a disused septic tank.

In fact, we don't know exactly where the bodies are buried. It also appears to be the case that there is a deep burial crypt beneath the ground close to where the mother and baby home was, so perhaps they are in there.

I focus on AP because the manner in which AP reported the story was typical. There was a rush to believe the worst about the nuns and about Catholic Ireland.

The fact that some terrible things did happen in Church-run institutions is no excuse whatsoever. Journalists are supposed to check facts. That is absolutely basic to journalism. Mistakes will obviously be made from time to time, but when a whole plethora of various serious mistakes are made in the one story, and I'm not just talking about AP here, then we've got a problem.

Why is there such a willingness to believe the very worst about Catholic Ireland? Why is there such an obsessive focus on the terrible things that sometimes happened here when terrible things, often of a similar nature happened in almost every country, many of them neither Catholic nor Christian?

Secular, Social Democratic Sweden often sterilised unmarried mothers over a four-decade period from 1935 until 1975 and sometimes made them have abortions. It also ran institutions.

As Dan O'Brien commented in the *Sunday Independent*, Switzerland effectively sold orphans to farmers as cheap labour. This happened until the 1950s.

In respect of Tuam, there were even earlier reports that the nuns were starving the babies and that many had died of malnutrition.

The Sunday Independent published a list of exactly how the 796 babies and young children died. Only a handful died of malnutrition. Those who did may well have arrived in the home already severely malnourished or had badly malnourished mothers.

The rest died of highly infectious diseases like measles which would often kill a dozen babies in the space of a fortnight. From the late 1940s when antibiotics came on stream, the death rate plunged.

The government has announced it is to hold an inquiry into the mother and baby homes. Hopefully it will be far more sober and balanced than much of the appalling reporting on this story that has taken place.

CHAPTER 49

WHY SHOULD IDEA OF STAYING CHASTE PROVOKE WAVE OF SHOCK AND AWE?

2014

It's a rare enough thing to live in a time when an old morality is turned exactly on its head with the result that what was once considered good is now considered bad and vice versa.

Nowhere is this effect stronger than in the realm of sexual morality. A previous generation would have been horrified at the idea of sex educationalists going into schools to teach teenagers how to put on a condom or to pass out free condoms.

Today, the idea that a group would go into schools with the message that you should wait until you're married before you have sex is more likely to cause the horrified reaction.

There is a Catholic organisation called Pure in Heart which goes into schools around the country with exactly this message and it has indeed been causing a horrified reaction over the last couple of weeks, in the media and on the internet at any rate.

To put it mildly, the idea that sex should wait until you're married is now radically counter-cultural whereas a few decades ago it was almost universally accepted.

People usually react in one of three ways to something that is genuinely counter-cultural.

The majority will simply dismiss the idea and not spare a further second's thought on it.

A minority might actually be intrigued and want to hear more. Another minority will react with complete fury precisely because they fear some people might be intrigued by this never-before-explained idea. They will seek to ban it.

This, of course, amounts to a call that Catholic groups teaching Catholic sexual morality should be banned from Catholic or any other schools, a rather extravagant proposition when you think about it.

It would make a whole lot more sense to ban non-Catholic groups from Catholic schools if what they teach is at odds with Catholic morality.

In fact, there is almost no pressure at all on Catholic schools to ban such groups – hence the 'how to wear a condom' lessons that sometimes take place – but there is now quite clearly a campaign to stop Catholic groups coming into Catholic schools to teach about chastity, and specifically to stop Pure in Heart.

The two basic objections to Pure in Heart – and to any chastity group indeed – are that their philosophy is offensive and unrealistic.

It's offensive because it is at the very least implicitly judgmental. The basic message, the critics say, is that unless you wait until you're married before you have sex you are somehow immoral.

It's unrealistic because who in this day and age is going to delay having sex until they're married?

But furthermore the message is dangerous, insist the critics, because it is also anti-contraception. If teenagers don't learn how to use contraceptives, they will be more likely to become pregnant or contract an STI.

Is the Pure in Heart message offensive by definition? In fact, in the final analysis, the only way to avoid giving any possible offence to anyone is to never attach morality to sex. We've gone a long way towards doing that already by reducing sexual morality to the basic principle that 'anything goes between consenting adults'.

If you even amend that to 'anything goes between consenting adults so long as you're in love', you're already 'judging' lots of people because lots of people who have sex don't care for one another in the slightest. But whatever about teaching teenagers that they should wait until they're married before they should have sex, don't parents want their children taught some kind of sexual morality that goes beyond the 'anything goes between consenting adults' line? Do they really want their teenagers to completely detach sex from any kind of relational or moral context? I doubt it. Pure in Heart's message is simply that sex belongs in the ultimate emotional and relational context, namely marriage.

Is this message 'unrealistic'? If it is, it's because our social and moral norms have changed so drastically that even those who do want to wait until they're married will often have a very hard time finding a partner who is also willing to wait.

One reason Pure in Heart exists is to tell those who want to wait that there is an organisation of like-minded young people out there who believe in the same things that they do. And indeed out there in the real world there are some people who do still wait until they're married and do manage to meet someone who feels the same way.

What about Pure in Heart's message about contraception? Again, it comes down to this; do Catholics have a right to teach the Catholic Church's message about contraception in Catholic schools?

Just as there are still some people who do actually wait until they are married before they have sex, so too there are people who don't use artificial contraception and successfully use natural forms of family planning instead. Is this message also so outrageous that teenagers must not hear it from inside the four walls of a classroom?

The single most cherished value of modern, liberal societies is choice. If we are really committed to choice, then we ought to be much more tolerant of the choice to marry before you have sex and be a lot more willing to let teenagers hear about this choice. Only a small minority might listen to the message, but they ought to be given that chance.

CHAPTER 50

AT SOME POINT, CHRISTIANITY HERE BECAME MORE ABOUT PUNISHMENT THAN FORGIVENESS

2014

Other countries are able to be nostalgic about their past. Britain can have the *Darling Buds of May*, which romanticises rural life in England in the 1950s. *Call the Midwife* is also set in the 1950s, this time in east London, but it is still fairly nostalgic about the past.

America has lot of films and TV shows that romanticise the 1950s. I don't think we have any. Instead we have lots of films that do the opposite and I think a huge part of the reason is that we are still haunted by the fact that we put so many people into mostly Church-run institutions that were often inhuman and dehumanising.

Britain also had its institutions and they were also terrible places. But we seemed to have more of them, we put proportionately more people into them and we kept them open until closer to the present day.

Another example of the awfulness of many of our institutions has just come to light, namely the fact that almost 800 children and babies have died at a Tuam mother and baby home run by an order of nuns between 1925 and 1961.

Eight hundred deaths means that a child was dying at an average rate of almost one a fortnight for the entire period. That is horrendous.

We have to determine how they died and where they are buried. Notably, the gardaí told RTÉ's Philip Boucher-Hayes concerning the burials at the home itself, a former workhouse: "They are historical burials going back to Famine times, there is no suggestion of any impropriety and there is no garda investigation. Also there is no confirmation from any source that there are there are between 750 and 800 bodies present."

The institutions were partly a response to extreme poverty. Destitute people often ended up in institutions as an alternative to being on the street. Go to a Third World country today and you will find the streets of their towns and cities teeming with children many of whom belong to the sort of gangs depicted by Dickens in *Oliver Twist.*

Keep those countries in mind and you have a vision of how extreme poverty was in Ireland until fairly recently. In real terms, the Irish economy in 1936 was only one twelfth the size it was in 2007. That means many people were as poor then as some of the worst-off people in some of the worst-off African countries today.

The mortality rates and life expectancy for Irish people were also at Third World levels.

On average in the 1920s, almost 6,500 children aged up to four died annually. In 2010, 316 children in that age group died, a decrease of 95%. And the population of Ireland was much smaller in the 1920s than it is today.

The Bethany Children's Home was similar to the one in Tuam and to others all over the country. It was also a terrible place as has been highlighted by the tireless work of former resident, Derek Leinster.

It too had a terrible mortality rate and it too had its unmarked graves. One, in Mount Jerome cemetery, had 40 bodies buried in it in 1935 and 1936 alone.

Because it was Protestant-run and there is no extant institution that claims responsibility for it – church or state – it never came under the Residential Institutions Redress Board.

Commenting on the Bethany Home in the Dáil in late 2013, Labour party TD and Minister of State at the Department of Justice, Kathleen Lynch said: "The number of children who died at Bethany Home is quite shocking. Unfortunately, poverty and disease were commonplace in Ireland up to the 1950s and this was reflected in infant mortality rates. Infant mortality rates in the 1940s were at a level that are hard to comprehend today, about

20 times higher than now and that figure applies across the entire population. For those who were malnourished and subject to disease and a lack of hygiene the figures would have been higher still."

Lynch, responding to a motion from Sinn Féin, concluded her speech: "As I have said earlier the infant mortality rate in Bethany Home was very high by today's standards and children there did suffer from diseases associated with poverty and neglect. However, it seems to have been accepted at the time that Bethany Home was run by people with charitable motives.

"Did Bethany Home improve the lot of those who passed through its doors or did it make their lives worse by the standards that existed at the time?

"I am not here to defend those who ran Bethany Home but I am certainly not in a position to condemn them out of hand in the way proposed by Sinn Féin."

This reasoning seems pretty sound and some of it may apply to the home in Tuam. But even if we accept it, at bottom there was still something completely unacceptable about many of these places which, for all of their ostensible Christianity, were rarely Christian.

Why didn't the children and adults encounter a proper Christian witness, real love, when they walked through their doors? Why was it impersonal rules and regulations on a good day and cruelty of a sometimes very extreme kind on other days?

I think it was because Christianity in Ireland had by then hardened into something that was all too often more about punishment than mercy and forgiveness. To that extent Christianity in Ireland had become, in the strict meaning of the term, anti-Christ, and the Church is still living this down.

CHAPTER 51

THE TERRIBLE LOSS OF MY FRIEND, TOM O'GORMAN

2014

It has been a revelation to find out exactly how many people Tom O'Gorman knew. I was aware he had a wide circle of friends and acquaintances but not that it ran into hundreds upon hundreds.

Apart from Ireland, he had friends in America, Italy and Britain. Come to think of it, he was born in Scotland and I used to teasingly tell him he was really Scottish. In fact, he was a very proud Irishman.

He was even more crestfallen than the average rugby fan when we lost to New Zealand recently. It was like he had lost personally. He was absolutely over the moon when we won the Grand Slam for the first time in decades in 2009.

But to return to his friends, one after another has posted moving tributes or memories of Tom on both his and their own Facebook page including people who had diametrically opposed politics to Tom's. Some remembered him from his days in UCD, a place he adored.

One friend, a member of the Labour party, wrote: "Tom O'Gorman was a man I rarely agreed with politically, but he was always friendly and a gentleman, even when we stridently disagreed with one another. To think that he died in such a way is appalling. I am quite shocked."

Another person he knew from his time in UCD posted: "Tom was indeed a gentleman, kind, decent fellow. I did not always share his political views nor indeed his religious ones... I always liked him personally, it was hard not to... He is part of my great memories of my UCD student days."

Unfortunately, it is a very human trait to see your political opponents simply as political opponents and nothing else, especially if you never meet them socially. This is dehumanising, of course. We need always to remember that those we are opposed to politically and ideologically, even if they are completely at the other end of the spectrum from us, are fellow human beings.

Twitter, which is often a cesspit, put aside ideological differences this week and simply recognised that something mind-bogglingly awful had happened to Tom. I only saw one tweet that gloated over his death and I sincerely hope Twitter will block the person responsible.

On Tuesday night, a prayer vigil was conducted for Tom in St Teresa's, Clarendon St, in Dublin city centre. The choice of venue was apt because Tom often went there after work.

Hundreds turned up. I didn't recognise the vast majority of them, which again is testament to all the people Tom knew.

It was also indicative of the fact that he was anything but a loner. He was always seeking people out.

I remember on occasion when we were walking down the street together he would stop and have a quick chat with a homeless person he had gotten to know.

Tom has been described in various outlets as 'deeply religious'. But that can be misleading because it can easily give the impression that he was a 'Holy Joe'. Nobody who knew him would ever call him that. He didn't wear his religion on his sleeve and he wasn't in the least bit pious in the worst sense of that word.

He had an offbeat sense of humour. On the wall above his desk he had pinned various pictures and posters that illustrated it. My favourite was the 'National Sarcasm Society', which said: 'Like we need your support.'

He also had Martin Luther King's 'I have a dream' pinned above his desk, showing another side of him.

On his bookshelf he had numerous books dealing with politics and history. He had *The Blair Years* by Alastair Campbell; *India After Gandhi*; and *A History of Modern Russia*' among others. They illustrated his range of interests.

I've since discovered that he had different friends who reflected his different tastes. He'd talk about rugby and football with people who shared those interests. He talked about his musical tastes with some, and films with others. Obviously, he loved to talk about politics and he knew a lot about ordinary, day-to-day party politics.

His interest in politics extended to Britain and America and he had a lot of American friends. Some of them have organised a memorial service for him in Washington DC. He would have been enormously touched by that.

He would also have been very touched by Tuesday night's vigil and the excellent tribute that was paid to him by his long-time friend, Joe McCarroll. What was notable at the vigil, incidentally, is that there wasn't one word of anger directed at his killer. The only person on people's minds was Tom.

For all who knew him, the last few days have been utterly surreal. It is very hard to absorb the enormity of the evil that befell him.

The whole nation is shocked by it, and not just Ireland. My sister in New Zealand heard it reported there because Tom's death was so uniquely horrific.

To be honest, I'm not really sure how you process something like this. What happened to him is so shocking it is almost uncharted territory. However, everybody who knew him has happy memories of him. Thankfully, these memories will eventually supplant in their minds the terrible manner of his death.

CHAPTER 52

GOVERNMENT'S EXPERIMENT WITH THE LIVES OF IRELAND'S CHILDREN IS A SCANDAL

2015

The most radical piece of family law reform in the history of the State is currently before the Oireachtas. It is being rushed through our parliament on the nod with the full cooperation of the Opposition.

The Children and Family Relationships Bill completely upends what most people think of when they hear the word 'family'.

When your average person hears this word, they think of mother, father and child. They think of brothers and sisters and cousins and uncles and aunts and grandparents.

Everyone knows that circumstances such as the death of a parent or the divorce of a child's parents can alter this picture, this image people have in their minds. Nonetheless, it is what most people think of when they hear the word 'family'.

The government has something different in mind entirely. The government is keen to facilitate people who want to radically change what the word 'family' means.

How does it mean to do this? Here's how. Both the government and the opposition want to facilitate people who wish to deliberately cut the tie between a child and his or her natural parent or parents through the use donor eggs and/or sperm.

They want to facilitate and enable people who wish to deliberately deprive a child of a mother or a father by the same means, a single man or woman say, or a same-sex couple.

They want to deliberately facilitate and enable people to use the sperm or eggs or womb of family members in order to have a child and in so doing deliberately confuse family relationships.

What do I mean by this? Here's an example. The British media gave some attention a couple of weeks ago to the case of Mary Portas, a minor celebrity who is in a lesbian relationship. Her partner has become pregnant with sperm from Portas's brother.

What does this mean? It means that the child's 'uncle' will in fact be the child's father and it means that Portas herself, who will be the child's second 'mother', will actually be the child's aunt.

Fertility experts in the UK are quoted in the papers as saying cases like this are becoming more common. They say they have come across cases where a mother donates an egg to an infertile daughter so she can have a child with her partner.

This means the daughter will in fact be giving birth to her half-sibling, her husband will be having a child via his mother-in-law and the mother-in-law will at one and the same time be the child's grandmother and biological mother. Her daughter will be the child's birth mother and, as mentioned, half-sister.

Confused? If you are, imagine how confused the child will be. Their absolutely normal expectation of who is who within their extended family will have been deliberately confounded. This is terribly wrong.

In the UK papers this week is the case of a woman who gave birth to a child conceived via IVF on behalf of her single son. So the son's mother is also the birth mother of his child as well as being the grandmother of the child.

Commenting on this, Labour MP, Robert Flello, said: "This case throws up many concerns and worries. My greatest concern in all of this is the po-tential emotional damage to the child in years to come, as he tries to work out family relationships that most of us can take for granted." Precisely.

What has this got to do with the Children and Family Relationships Bill? Everything. The Bill permits people to have children using the sperm or eggs of other family members and thereby deliberately mix up who is a child's aunt, who is a child's uncle, who is a child's mother, or birth mother, or grandmother. It creates situation whereby someone can be both the mother of a child and the grandmother, the uncle and the father, the aunt and the mother.

Indeed, the Institute of Obstetricians and Gynaecologists admitted in a statement last week that even now family members are giving sperm or eggs to other family members so they can have children.

Our government could outlaw this practice, but it hasn't and it won't.

The Bill also permits two women to be recorded on a birth cert as the parents of a child. The father's name won't be recorded. A birth cert is supposed to be a record of who the natural parents of a child are. Two women cannot both be the natural parents of the one child and yet their names will both be recorded on birth certs in the future.

This is the deliberate falsification of an official document in the name of political correctness. It is ideology trumping nature.

How can Frances Fitzgerald, Enda Kenny, Joan Burton, etc., possibly stand over this? Justice Minister Frances Fitzgerald would tell us she is merely reflecting reality. Actually, she is encouraging adults to deliberately scramble the genealogies of children.

It is simply unethical of the government to allow birth certs to be falsified in this way. It is unethical to allow IVF to be used to bring into existence a child who will be raised by two women and no father, or two men and no mother, or one parent alone and no parent of the opposite sex.

Remember, we are not talking here about a child losing a mother or a father by circumstance. We are talking about adults believing they have a right to deliberately deprive a child of a mother or a father with the full and express approval of the State, and to deliberately cut the natural tie between parent and child and to deliberately confound normal family relationships.

In other words, the government is embarked on a bold and irresponsible experiment on the lives of children and the very meaning of family and they are doing so with almost no debate.

That is a scandal.

CHAPTER 53

PROTECTING THE CONSCIENCE RIGHTS OF RELIGIOUS BELIEVERS

2015

Following off-the-cuff remarks made by Archbishop Diarmuid Martin at a meeting of The Iona Institute last week, the issue of a conscience clause for those who do not believe in same-sex marriage and do not wish to facilitate same-sex weddings has surfaced again.

Archbishop Martin did not expressly call for a conscience clause – that is not his style – but he did seem to give strongly backing to the notion of conscience rights.

Responding to a question, he wondered out loud why it was that religious solemnisers will not be forced to celebrate same-sex marriages but nothing similar exists for lay Christians.

He remarked: "What is this saying? It's saying, yes, there is a conscientious question and we respect the conscience of priests. But what about the lay Christian in the same difficulties – does he not have freedom of conscience? Is his conscience different to mine as a priest? I don't believe so."

Tiernan Brady of the Gay and Lesbian Equality Network dismissed any possibility of a conscience clause out-of-hand. He said it would like giving opt-outs to white racists.

Former Fianna Fáil Minister Pat Carey, who recently came out as gay, dismissed the idea on the grounds that we are now a 'mature, pluralist democracy'. (Why don't 'mature' democracies make provision for people's conscience rights?)

The emergence of conscience rights as an issue in the marriage referendum happened in the same week that the case of Ashers Bakery went before the courts in Northern Ireland.

A few months ago Ashers refused to bake a cake because the customer wanted it to bear a slogan in support of same-sex marriage. The owners of Ashers are Christians and so they refused. Even though same-sex marriage does not even exist in the North, the Northern Ireland Equality Commission took a civil case against them.

Ashers is being backed by the Christian Institute in the UK. The Christian Institute commissioned an opinion poll to coincide with the court hearing this week.

It found that only 27% of Northern Irish adults think it is right for the Equality Commission to take Ashers to court, while 71% disagree.

And 77% believe the commission should not be spending public funds pursuing Ashers through the courts.

Respondents, who were from all faiths and none, were given various scenarios and asked whether they should be grounds for taking someone to court. The poll showed that:

- Over three quarters (79%) believe a Muslim printer should not be taken

  to Court for refusing to print cartoons of the Prophet Mohammed.
- Over eight in 10 (82%) believe an atheist web designer should not be forced by the Courts to design a website promoting the view that God made the world in six days.
- Almost three quarters (74%) believe a printing company run by Roman Catholics should not be forced by legal action to produce adverts calling for abortion to be legalised.

A legal opinion commissioned by the Christian Institute said that if the court finds against Ashers then printers faced with the above scenarios would have to print off anything the customer wanted regardless of their own beliefs. In other words, conscience would count for little or nothing.

Supporters of same-sex marriage have insisted all along that allowing same-sex marriage will harm no one and will simply allow two people who love each other to get married. We now know that this is untrue. If we permit same-sex marriage than anyone with a different view could be treated under law as the equivalent of a racist bigot.

In other words, the view of practically all of humanity to this day, that marriage is the union of a man and a woman (or more than one woman where polygamy is permitted), will be seen as so completely unreasonable that in certain circumstances it should be punishable under law by fines or even imprisonment.

Of course, opponents of a conscience clause will claim that until relatively recent times most of humanity believed in slavery. But there is the extreme comparison again. Is believing that marriage is by definition the union of a man and a woman really the same as believing in slavery?

Is believing children ought to be raised by their own mother and father (a belief that has always attached to the age-old view of marriage) really the same as believing in slavery?

Comparisons like this in fact make very clear what the end game of many same-sex marriage supporters is; they want to make belief in man/woman marriage and in motherhood and fatherhood as unacceptable as racism.

This is why the debate over same-sex marriage is so incredibly high stakes.

Over time, as the view that believing in the 'traditional' family is equivalent to racism takes hold, the law will become more and more intolerant of those who continue to hold to it.

In many cases those people will be religious believers whether Christian, Jewish, Muslim, Hindu and so on.

They will increasingly be forced to keep their views on the family and marriage to themselves and they will be effectively barred from any business that has anything to do with weddings if they do not wish to facilitate same-sex marriages.

Over time, the pressure may even be applied to religious celebrants to perform same-sex marriage ceremonies. Archbishop Martin has a point when he asks why religious celebrants should have their conscience rights protected and not lay Christians.

The trouble is that eventually the State may conclude not that both should have their conscience rights protected, but that neither should.

CHAPTER 54

THE OLD SEXUAL NORMS COULD BE CRUEL BUT SO CAN THE NEW ONES

2015

One of the books I'm currently reading is called *In the Family Way: Illegitimacy Between the Great War and the Swinging Sixties*, by Jane Robinson. The title is self-explanatory. It looks mainly at how illegitimate children and their mothers were dealt with in Britain in the period in question, but also has a look at Ireland.

To cut a long story short, for the most part these children and their mothers were dealt with cruelly, and sometimes extremely so.

It's interesting, by the way, to read in detail how organisations like Barnardos and the Salvation Army did their best according to their lights to ensure that the children and their mothers were dealt with less harshly than many in society wanted.

In a column for *The Sunday Independent* recently, Gene Kerrigan condemned what he called 'the marriage police' and how liberal campaigners saved us from them.

There is not the slightest doubt that the norms around marriage were sometimes very harshly enforced, and not just here, but in many other countries also.

We were determined to ensure that children were only born within marriage and woe betide the person who broke that rule, and woe betide their children. It was believed that the only way to keep rates of illegitimacy down was to make an example both of the mothers and their offspring. It worked insofar as only a small minority of children were born out of wedlock until comparatively recent times, but at what a cost.

So liberal campaigners did indeed rescue women and children from those harsh and punitive attitudes.

However, to think that the only two alternatives we face are between the harsh attitudes of the past and the present one that seems to say marriage hardly matters at all is false and misleading. We have to find a way of saying marriage matters, and that it benefits children to be raised by their own mothers and fathers, without returning to the former cruelty.

We can concede that the norms we created around marriage in the past were extreme, but we also need to be honest about the failing of liberal morality when applied to marriage, sex and human relationships. If traditionalism can lead to the harsh enforcement of certain norms, the liberal attachment to notions of 'autonomy' and 'freedom' can lead to a sort of normlessness, a world without any rules to speak of, and this also ill serves people.

There is, of course, one great liberal rule that is applied to sex and human relationships and it is this; anything goes between consenting adults. But a report came out in England a couple of weeks ago that shows where this can lead.

The report concerns the city of Oxford. It details how a gang was allowed to sexually exploit and abuse 300 girls, some as young as 12.

This was happening right under the noses of social workers, police, doctors and nurses. How can this have happened?

The report explains that there was a reluctance to condemn underage sex as "wrong". It says there was a "well-meaning" desire to be "non-judgemental".

As *The Daily Telegraph* reports: "It criticised a widespread belief that the children's 'self-determining choice' should be respected in sexual matters, pointing specifically to the way contraception is readily distributed to girls from a young age."

It said that there is a "professional tolerance" to underage sexual activity in a culture "where children are sexualised at an ever younger age."

In other words, it is precisely the liberal commitment to the notion of freedom that helped to land these girls in such trouble at the hands of older men.

The social workers etc.. wanted to the "non-judgemental". They believed the children's "self-determining choice" should be respected in sexual matters.

Then there is the fact that the surrounding culture has become so heavily sexualised that people are having sex for the first time at younger and younger ages and in response to this school nurses are handing out contraception to young people who are often well below the age of consent.

This blurs the whole notion of an age of consent, and who can and cannot be considered an 'adult' for sexual purposes.

And so we have a complete mess that leaves younger people wide open to sexual exploitation at the hands of older adults with social workers, police and doctors so determined to be 'open-minded' and 'tolerant' that they turn a blind eye.

In response the British government has announced that children as young as 11 will have to be taught the difference between rape and consensual sex because the line between the two is sometimes so blurred especially when drink is involved.

This isn't confined to children either. American universities, for example, are going beyond 'No means No' to advocating that unless there is explicit consent to sex, any sex that occurs can be considered rape.

The British Director of Public Prosecutions, Alison Saunders has said something similar recently.

What we are seeing is the strain that even the minimalist sexual morality embodied in 'anything goes between consent adults' is coming under when the notion of who is an 'adult' and what is 'consent' is becoming so blurred.

The norms that existed around sexual morality in the past were cruelly enforced but the new sexual morality is producing huge problems of its own from very high levels of family breakdown, to high levels of abortion, to the sort of sexual exploitation of children found in Oxford, and a few months ago, in Rochdale.

It should be clear to any sensible person that what we need is a balance between the old norms that took marriage seriously and the new norms (such as they are) that has placed freedom above any other value.

CHAPTER 55

UNREALISTIC EXPECTATIONS SPELL TROUBLE FOR MODERN MARRIAGES

2015

When my parents married in 1958 they got married in the morning, had a lunch-time wedding reception for a few dozen people and were gone by mid-afternoon. My mother didn't wear a wedding dress. Instead, she wore a white suit consisting of a skirt and jacket. Apparently, it was common back then not to wear a wedding dress.

Even if you translate what they paid for their wedding into today's money, it must have been a fraction of what is forked out nowadays.

The *Irish Independent* has been running a series of articles about marriage in Ireland today, which estimates that the average Irish couple now spends a little over €20,000 on their big day.

We're led to believe that marriage in Ireland is more popular than ever. It's easy to point to official figures from the CSO showing that more Irish people than ever are getting married.

But looking at the absolute numbers only is misleading. Of course, more Irish than ever are getting married because our population is the biggest it has been since the middle of the 19th Century - and a big proportion of us are currently of 'marrying age', which for brides these days is around 33 and for grooms around 35.

The rate of marriage, however, is much lower than it was in the 1970s and 1980s - at around 4.5 people per thousand getting married each year.

This is down about 40% compared with 1973, when the marriage rate peaked.

Prior to the mid-1960s, Ireland had an unusually low marriage rate, one of the lowest in Europe, in fact. This can be put down to two big factors: the first is that so many Irish of marrying age emigrated, and the second is the legacy of the Famine - which resulted in people delaying getting married until they were financially secure.

As we became relatively more prosperous from the mid-1960s on, our marriage rate started to climb because emigration dipped and because people felt financially secure enough to marry at younger ages. In the 1980s, the average bride was around 24 and the average groom was around 27.

Now our marriage rate has dipped again, so much so that it has fallen below the levels seen in the early 1960s. The difference is that this time our marriage rate is not out of line with the sort of rate seen in other European countries. That's because the rate in most of Europe is now very low by historical standards.

What's driving down the marriage rate? Several things - one is the delay in getting married, another is the rise of cohabitation as a substitute for marriage, instead of being something that comes before marriage.

Cohabitation isn't a substitute for marriage on the scale it is in countries like France or Sweden, but we're getting there, especially in working class areas. The fact is that the middle class are more likely to marry than people from disadvantaged areas.

Another fact that belies the 'marriage is more popular than ever' line is the rise in divorce and separation. Again, we're nowhere near what we see in the likes of Britain or America. Nonetheless, according to census figures there was 40,000 separated people in Ireland in 1986, but by 2011 this had risen to a quarter of a million. That is a big absolute total.

Sociologists say we are moving from 'institutional marriage' to 'companionate marriage' to the 'individualised marriages' of today.

In the days of institutional marriages, when you married, the marriage was less about you and more about the social institution you had entered. Marriage meant you had entered into a contract with society as well as each other. Your job was to keep your building block of society from falling apart. Once married, you stayed married come what may.

Companionate marriage was more about the couple - and your 'contract' with society was less important.

Individualised marriage brings the whole process to its logical conclusion. Sociologist, Andrew Cherlin, explains what this means, saying: "When people evaluated how satisfied they were with their marriages, they began to think more in terms of the development of their own sense of self and the expression of their feelings, as opposed to the satisfaction they gained through building a family and playing the roles of spouse and parent.

"The result was a transition from the companionate marriage to what we might call the individualised marriage."

One wedding organiser quoted recently noted how couples are now much more inclined to tailor their wedding day to their individual tastes and to come up with their own wedding vows. Going along with tradition for its own sake is out.

But the individualism that permeates the wedding day is now a lot more likely to permeate the entire marriage. Most of us now think it's a good thing that society no longer forces people to stay married no matter how unhappy they are. There is a long way from that, however, to the current situation - whereby lots of people pull the plug on their marriage, not because they are desperately unhappy, but because they are not as happy as they expected to be.

A friend once told me that a friend of hers had divorced, not because she was particularly unhappy, but because she wasn't 'happy, happy'. What marriage could possibly survive this kind of pressure and expectation?

According to recent American research, at least half of marriages that end in divorce are low-conflict marriages.

That is, the couples don't have regular heated arguments, or worse. When the couple sit their children down to tell them the bad news, the children are often blissfully unaware that their parents were headed for the divorce courts, because there were few visible signs of conflict between them.

Research also shows that couples who stick at it through the tough patches very often come out the other side again, and the marriage survives.

Here in Ireland, we seem to be at the mid-way point between institutional marriage and individualised marriage. That is, we're at the companionate stage. Hence, our fairly low marital breakdown rate.

However, if the very individualised nature of the modern Irish wedding starts to mean very individualised marriages – and we place unrealistic expectations on them – then we're in trouble.

CHAPTER 56

ENDA KENNY KILLS OFF LAST TRACES OF FINE GAEL'S CHRISTIAN DEMOCRACY

2015

When Enda Kenny took up the office of Taoiseach four years ago this week, those of us with 'traditionalist' views knew we were in for a bumpy ride, but we never anticipated it would be as violently bumpy as it has been.

We knew that a coalition government that included Labour would make certain demands on the social issues. We could have guessed that a marriage referendum would be on the cards, for example, and that Catholic schools would find themselves in the firing line.

But what we never imagined is that Kenny would take to Labour's social issues agenda with such gusto. For example, we never imagined in a million years that he would preside over the closing of the Irish embassy to the Holy See or deliver that swingeing attack on the Vatican at the end of his first Dáil term.

Even Labour didn't expect that. No country in living memory had closed down its embassy to the Holy See in a fit of anger. No Western leader in living memory, not even the fanatically anti-clerical government of José Luis Rodríguez Zapatero (Spanish Prime Minister from 2004 to 2011) did such a thing.

The closing of the embassy and the attack on the Vatican were prompted by the report into abuse in the Cloyne diocese. That report showed how the diocese was failing to deal with reports of child abuse - almost all of them historical - in the way it should have. Bishop John Magee had previously - and rightly - resigned as a result of the failings.

However, the attack on the Vatican was still extraordinary, as was the decision to close our embassy to the Holy See.

Other countries had witnessed clerical child abuse scandals, including America, Britain, Canada and Australia. But none of them had closed their embassy to the Holy See and none had seen their leader launch such an attack on the Vatican.

Then again, the Catholic Church in those countries was never anything like as dominant as it was here. I think that partly explains why Kenny reacted as he did.

But it only partly explains it.

He never would have delivered that speech if he feared a significant public backlash or a significant media backlash. That's why it wasn't as brave as a lot of commentators suggested. Bravery is when you're willing to act on a point of principle regardless of the cost.

This is why Lucinda Creighton and the other politicians who lost the Fine Gael party whip in 2013 for voting against the abortion bill are much braver. They did pay a price for their actions.

That abortion bill was the next big surprise the government had in store for us.

Fine Gael explicitly promised that it would not legislate for abortion on the grounds of the X-case ruling of 1992. It won pro-life votes on this basis.

It claimed that the promise was made before the European Court of Human Rights declared that our law on abortion lacked clarity. But the promise was made after that.

The fact is that Fine Gael allowed itself to be bumped into legislating for abortion on the ground of a threat of suicide because it was bumped into it by the tragic death of Savita Halappanavar (from blood poisoning), by the Labour party, from its own liberal members, and by the media.

For good measure, no opt-out for Catholic hospitals was allowed. Catholic hospitals like the Mater and St Vincent's in Dublin must perform abortions under the terms of the new abortion law.

This is extreme. It is commonplace around the world for even publicly-funded Catholic hospitals to be exempted from having to perform abortions.

Kenny's government was once more determined that the State would put the Church in its 'place' to an extent found in few other countries.

Once again, Kenny was called 'brave' but there was no real price to be paid for his bravery, not in net terms anyway.

Fine Gael did lose seven members of the parliamentary party (one has since returned), and a few percentage points of support, but Kenny knew that if he didn't cave into the media, and to the Labour party, he would pay a bigger price down the road.

It hasn't stopped there. Kenny has been happy to see Labour go after Catholic schools, with other denominational schools being collateral damage.

The admissions policy of Catholic schools has been attacked. Their employment policy has been attacked. Their ethos has been attacked.

And of course, we have the *Children and Family Relationships Bill* and the upcoming marriage referendum.

The former is at the very far end of the liberal spectrum in its ideology. The later is essentially being shoved down our throats. How many voters really think the referendum is a high priority? Is it even 10%?

Enda has obviously become a convert to the 'modern family' view of things.

The 'modern family' is contrasted with the 'traditional family' which consists of mother, father and child. The former seems to be inclusive and non-judgemental, the latter more 'narrow' and 'rigid'.

But before we 'celebrate' the modern family too much, consider first that in many cases what makes a family 'modern' and 'non-traditional' is the absence of either the mother or the father.

It is the presence of both the mother and the father under the same roof that qualifies a family as 'traditional'.

The more 'modern' we become, therefore, the more children will grow up in households from which either the mother or the father is absent.

It is so strange. The European People's Party (EPP), the group in the European Parliament to which Fine Gael belongs, issued a statement on the family a few weeks ago that Pope Francis could have written. Maybe Enda should march Fine Gael out of the EPP in protest?

Fine Gael was once a Christian Democratic party. Under Enda Kenny it has left the last traces of that heritage behind.

Nor is it even very democratic. The ruthless use of the party whip and centralised control has seen to that.

Who would have believed that in four years as Taoiseach, Enda Kenny would lead his party, and the country, on such a march?

CHAPTER 57

STATE IS STILL FAILING TO PROTECT CHILDREN BUT WE DON'T SEEM TO CARE

2015

The extent to which this country really cares about child protection remains very much open to question. In 2012, a report was produced that reviewed the deaths of children who were either in the care of the State, or who were known to the State's care services, and why they died.

The *Report of the Independent Child Death Review Group* was published by the Minister for Children and Youth Affairs and was written by family law expert Geoffrey Shannon and Norah Gibbons of Barnardos.

What prompted it was the revelation that some 200 children in the care of the State had died in the previous ten years, many from natural causes, some by violence.

The admission that so many minors known to the State's care services were dead had to be dragged from the relevant authorities. When *The Sunday Business Post* first began to report on the matter, the initial response by the HSE was opaque. In this, it seemed very much like the Catholic Church.

Bit by bit, the true picture emerged until we finally found out that on average, 20 children per year die while in the care of the State, or while known to State services.

The Shannon/Gibbons Report looked into the various deaths and found that some of them were preventable. It was strongly critical of the State's performance in this regard.

It also found:
- The majority of children covered by the report did not receive an adequate child protection service;
- delays taking children into care;
- poor and incomplete records;
- failure to record critical incidents, including the deaths of almost 30 children;
- no care for young people after they turn 18;
- a lack of support and supervision for social workers.

The report made a whole series of recommendations. But things seem to have gotten even worse in the meantime.

Last week Tusla, also known as the Child and Family Agency, produced its annual report for 2014. Tusla is responsible for the State's child protection services.

It found that 26 children in the care of the State or who were known to the State's care services died last year. That is a record.

We can't simply blame Tusla for this increase. Maybe things are getting worse on the ground. Maybe the number of children in crisis situations is increasing and that accounts for the terrible new record.

That is not my immediate point, however. My immediate point is the lack of any real outcry. These latest figures were barely reported. What was mostly absorbing the attention of the media was the big pay-out to Pat Smith made by the IFA.

There was also a lack of any genuine outcry when the Shannon/Gibbons report was published. For the most part, it was inside page news, and not front-page news.

It was not discussed for days on end on all the big current affairs shows. No one had to resign. No one was held genuinely accountable.

We must contrast this with the massive coverage of all of the reports into clerical sex abuse when they were published.

Why there is such a contrast I will leave to your judgment. However, serious child protection failures by the State surely deserve more coverage than they get and surely there should be some accountability when a child protection failure is particularly egregious?

In Britain, social workers have sometimes had to resign over serious child protection failures. That has never happened here. Here, they are always able to hide behind the 'lack of resources' excuse, which is a genuine excuse but which can't be allowed to cover all sins.

Another report, this one issued on Tuesday, pulled back the curtain some more on why children end up in care in the first place. This report also received little coverage.

It is the final report of the 'Child Law Reporting Project' headed by Dr Carol Coulter. It examines over 1,000 cases of children who have come before the courts because of a failure of care on the part of their parents.

The biggest reason for a care order of some description being issued by the courts was a parental disability (176 out of the 1,074 cases examined).

Next came 'neglect', accounting for 164 cases. Parental drug abuse accounted for 136 cases, while drug abuse accounted for 115.

A total of 162 were removed from their parents for 'multiple' reasons.

Surprisingly (to me anyway), 'only' 36 children, or 3.6% of the total, were removed because of sexual abuse, and another 75 were removed because of physical and/or emotional abuse.

The report also looks at the family background of the children. It found that children from single-parent families, Traveller families and migrant families were over-represented in the cases that came before the courts compared with their numbers in the population.

One in four child protection cases involved families where at least one parent is an immigrant even though migrants make up 12% of the overall population.

Seventy-four percent of cases involved a parent who was parenting alone. Twenty-one percent of children overall are being raised by lone parents.

As the report puts it: "Parenting alone is difficult for anyone, even those of full ability and with strong social networks."

Another very important detail that caught the eye was the attitude of the Child and Family Agency (CFA) towards fathers.

When a child is removed from a mother, there is always the option of placing the child with its father, but this does not seem to happen as often as it should.

The report says: "... in a substantial minority of cases a father is involved in the [court] proceedings... However, the attitude of the CFA towards these fathers can sometimes be dismissive".

It then gives some examples of this.

Frankly, this is stunning. It shows a prejudice against fathers on the part of at least some State employees of the sort John Waters has been highlighting for years.

This prejudice, or dismissiveness, appears to run so deep in some cases that despite no evidence against the father who wishes to care for his child when the mother can't, the child is placed with strangers instead.

This is appalling, and we ought to be appalled by it. Given the fact, however, that child protection failures by the State still don't receive anything like the attention they deserve, we are unlikely to give the treatment of fathers by our courts the attention it deserves either. That is an injustice.

CHAPTER 58

IN OUR BRAVE NEW WORLD BOYS AND GIRLS ARE ABOLISHED BY DECREE

2015

At their 2015 annual conference, Britain's Liberal Democrats voted in favour of a motion calling for the removal of the terms 'male' and female' from official forms. This was done out of concern for transgendered or intersex people who might otherwise feel 'discriminated' against when confronted with gender categories they believe they don't fit into.

At some intervarsity debates here in Ireland, it is becoming common-place for speakers to first be asked to state the pronoun by which they wish to be identified. Just because you look like a man does not mean you wish to be identified as such. Perhaps you are really a woman.

The *New York Times* reports that a growing number of American schools have LGBTQQA clubs and when they meet, the members are asked what their 'PGP' is today. 'PGP' stands for 'preferred gender pronoun'. It might be 'Miss', 'Mr', 'Ms' or 'Mx'. 'Mx' is for those who identify neither as male nor female.

LGBTQQA incidentally, stands for 'Lesbian, Gay, Bisexual, Transsexual, Queer, Questioning and Allies'.

The *Boston Globe* reports that Harvard University now allows its students to choose from a whole range of gender pronouns including 'ze' and 'hir'. 'Ze' is halfway between 'he' and 'she', while 'hir' is halfway between 'him' and 'her'.

In Sweden, some crèches now encourage children to use gender-neutral pronouns. Some clothes shops in Sweden now mix boys' and girls' clothes together because there is no longer any such thing as 'boys' clothes' and 'girls' clothes'.

Facebook now allowed its users to choose from no fewer than 56 different genders ranging from Agender and Bigender to Cis Male and Cis Female, from Gender Fluid and Gender Variant to Intersex and Pansgender, from Trans Man and Trans Woman to Trans Male and Trans Female.

No, I don't know what all of these mean either.

Here's an insight though. In 2016, a Scottish group calling itself 'Free Pride' decided to ban drag queens from performing at its events. The reason? Drag queens hold up men who dress as women to ridicule and therefore offend transsexuals. They are therefore guilty of 'transphobia' and 'trans-misogyny'.

But then some transsexual drag queens objected. How could they be transphobic, they asked, when they are transsexuals themselves?

Free Pride promptly adjusted its policy to ban only 'cis-male' drag queens, namely drag queens who were 'assigned' the male gender at birth and still identify as male today.

In Sweden and Canada, we have had examples of parents who are raising their children in a 'gender-neutral' way. They have given them gender-neutral names and dress them in gender-neutral clothes so the people they meet cannot identify them as either male or female. A parent of one of these children said that it is not up to parents or society to "impose" a gender on children. Children must be allowed to choose their gender for themselves.

Welcome to the world of gender ideology. In this world, gender is not something we are born with. We either choose our gender or it is 'imposed' on us.

This is why these gender theorists insist that we are not born 'male' or 'female', except in the physical sense, but that we are 'assigned' one or other gender by the doctors and our parents at birth. From then on, the world insists on treating us as either 'male' or 'female' and this is what we become. We start to behave in 'stereotypically' 'male' or 'female' ways because we are dressed in 'boys' clothes' or 'girls' clothes'. We are given 'boys' toys' or 'girls' toys' and adults play with us in gentle ways if we are girls and rougher ways if we are boys.

Gender ideologues believe gender is a social construct, pure and simple. They believe male and female behaviours are not innate, not natural, but are taught to us by society: we become conditioned.

With different conditioning, they believe, women would be just as inclined to go to football matches (say) as men.

Needless to say, this theory is fantastically controversial. It runs smack into evidence that there are innate, natural differences between men and women that go beyond our physical bodies, even allowing for the fact that some men are more feminine than the average and some women are more masculine.

Controversial it may be, but it is now coming to a school near you, quite likely your child's school.

The Irish National Teachers' Organisation (INTO) now backs a programme for primary schools called 'Different Families, Same Love' which, among other things, will teach children in Junior Infants about transgenderism. Schools are reportedly to be asked to draw up new uniform rules for pupils who identify as transsexual.

This is already happening in a lot of American schools and it is causing ructions because it doesn't stop there. For example, boys who identify as girls must be allowed to use female toilets and female changing rooms. Many of the girls, backed by their parents, have objected to this.

Some schools have offered special changing rooms and toilets for trans-gendered pupils. Transgendered groups reject this. A boy who identifies as a girl must be allowed to use the facilities earmarked for girls.

In response, some schools are now beginning to make changing rooms and toilets 'gender-neutral' and are abandoning the terms 'male' and 'female' altogether.

Also, what happens to sports teams? Should boys who identify as girls be allowed to play on girls' teams? In some cases the answer has been 'yes'.

The Department of Education seems to believe that the needs of trans-gender pupils can be catered for without any kind of disruption being caused. That is completely unrealistic, as the American examples show.

Gender ideology at the end of the day wants us to think that the categories of 'male' and 'female' exist mostly in our heads and are not an absolutely intrinsic, basic and fundamental element of what it means to be human.

What beckons is a gender-neutral world of gender-neutral bathrooms and changing rooms, gender-neutral official forms and gender-neutral pronouns like 'ze' and 'hir'.

In a sense, the very categories of male and female are to be deemed bigoted and discriminatory.

This is the Brave New World we are now entering and children must be inculcated in it from the earliest possible age, without their parents being consulted about it in any meaningful way.

CHAPTER 59

THE NEXT GOAL FOR LIBERALS WILL BE REFERENDUM ON ABORTION

2015

Almost 750,000 people voted against the redefinition of marriage and the family last Friday. This is not far short of the popular vote won by Fine Gael in the General Election of 2011. It represents 38% of all those who voted.

I was hoping the 'no' vote would breach the 40% mark. I was dreading it dipping below the 30% mark. A victory for the 'no' side would have been the most stupendous upset in Irish political history.

But 750,000 voters is a lot of people and I was proud to help represent them. The government cannot now pretend they don't exist. Will it treat them with respect? Will it take any of their concerns into account in such areas of freedom of conscience or surrogacy?

It is amazing to think that so many people hadn't a single political party to represent them. Instead it fell to a handful of individuals from civic society and a handful of mostly independent politicians to do so.

Had even one of the major political parties backed the 'no' side, the number of people who voted 'no' would have swelled. It would have made a big difference to have the machinery of one of the main parties on our side. Not a decisive difference necessarily, but a difference.

It would also have helped to have a major media outlet on our side, especially one of the radio stations. Imagine if one of the national media organisations was on the No side?

It would be a useful exercise to properly survey those who voted 'yes' to find out their reasons for doing so. We would probably find that every one of them had voted 'yes' out of a sense of fairness.

But how many really believe that the biological ties between children and their parents don't really matter? How many really believe that mothers and fathers are interchangeable and that the differences between the sexes don't matter at all when it comes to raising children?

Some 62% of the electorate voted 'yes' on Friday, but opinions polls also consistently show that about the same number believe that children are best raised by a mother and father, all things being equal.

Obviously a lot of people didn't make a connection between that and changing Article 41 of the Constitution, which deals with the family.

It's disappointing that such a huge majority of people in working-class areas voted 'yes'. Is this a rebellion against the traditional family of mum and dad? If so, it's self-destructive.

Professor Robert Putnam, one of the world's leading academics and impeccably liberal in his credentials, has written a book called *Our Kids*. It deals with how our children will have fewer opportunities to get ahead in life than we have had, relatively speaking.

One reason for this, he says, is the breakdown of the traditional family in working-class parts of America compared with middle-class areas. The same thing is happening in Ireland.

Where does the 'liberal agenda' go to from here? The liberal agenda tries to advance individual freedom. The freedom to marry whoever you want (within certain limits) is part of that.

I believe this can come at the expense of other goods, in the case of same-sex marriage the good of having a mother and a father whenever possible.

In the case of divorce, we have seen the number of separated and divorced people climb in the space of 25 years from 40,000 in 1986 to 250,000 in 2011. That doesn't include all the children affected by this.

It is plain and obvious that abortion and assisted suicide are next on the agenda.

Liberals believe that women ought to have a choice about whether to bring a baby to term or to abort it.

They also believe that people ought to have the choice to end their own life at a time of their choosing, based on certain limitations.

The pressure to permit assisted suicide has been building for some time. Both have the support of many politicians and most of the media and a growing section of the public.

Assisted suicide will not require a referendum. It is entirely possible that the next government will make moves in favour of allowing assisted suicide in initially limited circumstances, to be widened over time.

I wouldn't be surprised if we have a referendum to remove the pro-life clause of our Constitution in the next two or three years. The issue of 'fatal foetal abnormalities' will be used to persuade the public to get rid of the Eighth Amendment.

Those seeking abortion will be hugely emboldened by what happened on Friday. At the same time, however, many politicians will know that the 38% of people who voted against same-sex marriage can be turned into a majority opposed to deleting the Eighth Amendment. Perhaps this will slow things down a little, but not for long.

CHAPTER 60

REPEALING THE EIGHTH WOULD QUICKLY LEAD TO ABORTION ON DEMAND

2015

When the World Meeting of Families, that may or may not include a visit by Pope Francis, takes place in Ireland in 2018, will we by then have repealed the protection that our Constitution gives to the unborn? The way things are going at present, the answer might, just might, be yes.

What a present for Pope Francis that would be.

Since the passage of the marriage referendum, many of the same groups that campaigned for it have been campaigning full throttle for an abortion referendum.

The same tactics are at play that we saw in the run-up to the marriage referendum. Feed to a compliant media lots of personal stories of women who have had abortions and paint your opponents in the blackest-possible colours, preferably as women-hating fundamentalists.

As in the marriage referendum, the aim is to create a spiral of silence, so that those who favour keeping the pro-life provisions of our Constitution intact dare not say so in public.

On this score, however, there was a significant enough straw in the wind this week, which shows that the spiral of silence has a long way to go before it matches what took hold before the marriage referendum.

Limerick City Council considered a motion calling for the repeal of the Eighth Amendment, that is to say, the pro-life amendment to our Constitution. By a two-to-one majority the councillors voted against the motion.

If Limerick City Council voted by two-to-one against a pro-abortion motion, what would happen in the county councils?

Long before the marriage referendum, the same-sex marriage lobby had the councils well and truly sown up.

Enda Kenny has not promised an abortion referendum and says he would not favour a liberal abortion regime himself.

Then again, he was once opposed to same-sex marriage and before the 2011 election Fine Gael said it would not introduce abortion legislation, then it went ahead and did so in 2013.

Enda, as usual, will go in whatever direction the wind pushes him. He will follow the line of least resistance.

Within his own party, very senior figures, such as Frances Fitzgerald and Leo Varadkar, favour repeal of the Eighth.

Fitzgerald has never supported that pro-life amendment. Varadkar, on the other hand, once did, but then performed one of his U-turns and now wants it repealed. What does he want it replaced with?

For its part, Labour has become bolder and bolder in its support for a liberal - which is to say permissive - abortion regime.

During the 2011 General Election campaign, I wrote a column in which I said that a vote for Labour was a vote for abortion. That was bluntly put and Michael D. Higgins appeared on Newstalk to blast me from a height.

As it turned out, I was absolutely correct - and sooner than I would have imagined. However, I did not anticipate that this government would introduce our first piece of abortion legislation after only two years in office.

Now Labour wants to go much further. It wants the Eighth Amendment repealed entirely and it has put two campaigners for a permissive abortion law in charge of what should replace it, namely Ivana Bacik and Sinéad Ahern.

Ahern is a member of Choice Ireland. The website of Choice Ireland tells us that one of its aims is "free and legal abortion on demand". Ahern is now head of Labour Women.

Abortion on demand means abortion for any reason whatsoever.

I actually think Labour has made a mistake putting Bacik and Ahern in charge of its abortion policy. Labour can no longer pretend to the electorate that its abortion policy is 'middle of the road'.

A Leo Varadkar-led campaign to repeal the Eighth would be much harder to deal with. He would be better at reassuring the public that whatever would replace the Eighth Amendment would be 'restrictive' in its effects, much more restrictive than what Britain has on its statute books. Pro-life groups would not be able to find any militantly pro-choice quotes from Leo that could be used against him in a campaign.

Dr Vicky Conway of Dublin City University said recently that the repeal of the Eighth Amendment would not create a legal vacuum. Indeed it would not, because what she has in mind for its replacement would be based on a private member's Bill called the 'Access to Abortion Bill'.

She describes this Bill as "lamentably conservative". She would like it to go much further. Look up the Bill. It is online. It goes quite far enough.

It allows for what amounts to abortion on demand up to 12 weeks of pregnancy.

The drafters of the Bill would vehemently deny this, of course. They would say this is far from abortion on demand because it requires that there be a threat to the health of the mother and this must be authenticated by two doctors.

But in Britain there must also be a 'threat' to the health of the woman and again two doctors must sign off on this. We all know, however, that in practice this has led to de facto abortion on demand.

There are almost 200,000 abortions in the UK each year.

It would be interesting to know what Leo Varadkar thinks of this Bill. He told the Dáil last year that he favours repeal of the Eighth because he believes it does not protect the "long-term health" of women. So there is the health ground again, just as in the UK.

It cannot be emphasised strongly enough that Ireland without a permissive abortion regime is at least as safe a place for women to have a baby as Britain with its permissive regime.

Therefore, we do not need to introduce a 'health' ground for abortion in order to protect pregnant women. But if we do introduce a health ground, de facto abortion on demand is what we will have in short order.

This, then, is the choice that we face. If the Eighth Amendment is repealed, nothing will stand in the way of some future government liberalising our abortion law in any way it chooses. It would no longer have to refer the matter back to the people.

Those calling for the repeal of the Eighth are admitting that they want to see abortion permitted in Ireland on very wide grounds. They want to see a British-style abortion regime introduced to Ireland.

This is what will be at stake in any future abortion referendum.

There is nothing 'moderate' about that aim.

CHAPTER 61

WOULD THE REAL THOMAS MORE PLEASE STAND UP?

2015

Most readers will probably have seen the movie *A Man for All Seasons* at one point or another in their lives.

Released in 1966 it was based on the Robert Bolt play of the same name. Paul Schofield played Thomas More as a man of deep conviction, erudition, patient in the face of adversity, kind and attentive to his family, dutiful, and finally prepared to face death rather than betray his conscience.

Thomas Cromwell, on the other hand, who succeeded More as Henry's right-hand man, is conniving, ruthlessly ambitious, and an ignoble character compared with the noble More.

More is, of course, a saint of the Church, and the patron saint of politicians into the bargain. Few politicians will even lose the party whip, let alone face death for what they believe, and while More was not a politician as such, the role of Lord Chancellor was deeply political. When Henry told More to sign the Oath of Supremacy and recognise Henry as head of the new Church of England the easy thing to do would have been to sign it.

After all, almost every bishop in England had signed it and so had the nobility. Why was Thomas More being so stubborn? Why could he not be 'reasonable'?

Even Alice, More's wife, wrote in a letter to Henry that he was in the grip of 'devilish fantasy' and therefore not responsible for his actions. Henry would have none of it and Alice probably didn't believe it either but was desperately trying to free her husband from the sentence of death.

It is worth bearing in mind that although More was beheaded in the end, for a long time he was in danger of being hanged, drawn and quartered, a truly hideous death.

Mainly as a result of *A Man for All Seasons* we tend to think well of Thomas More. But Hilary Mantel has other ideas. She clearly dislikes More's exalted reputation and wants to tear it down.

Mantel is the author of two historical novels about More's protagonist, Thomas Cromwell, *Wolf Hall* and *Bring Up the Bodies*. Both of these novels have been condensed into a new six-part drama for the BBC called *Wolf Hall*. It is being rightly praised as a very fine piece of television.

In any event, what Mantel has done is to swap the personalities and characters of More and Cromwell as commonly depicted.

Cromwell becomes the man of noble character and More the conniver, a hypocrite and a religious fanatic who wore a hair shirt in order to 'mortify the flesh' and sent heretics to the stake.

Mantel is a convent-educated girl who has since become a vociferous critic of the Catholic Church. Her attitude towards More fits in with this.

Is Mantel's criticism of More correct? I'm not a historian, let alone an expert on the period in question. I will instead refer you to *The Life of Thomas More* by Peter Ackroyd, which is regarded as the best biography of More.

Ackroyd is not a religious believer and therefore has no partisan reason to extol the virtues of More. Nonetheless, the More which emerges from his book is not too far off the More found in *A Man for All Seasons*.

The More Ackroyd describes is deeply admirable, the most educated man in the land, a Christian humanist, pious in the manner of other pious late Medieval people, a family man who thought his daughter should be as educated as any man, and a devoted servant of God and King until he believed the King had set himself against God by splitting from the Pope and Rome.

But the real lesson of Mantel's revisionist depiction of More and Cromwell is this; a historian and a novelist can use history as so much putty. Think of a recent figure like Margaret Thatcher. She has fierce critics and devoted followers. A critic would turn a historical novel about her into an attack. An admirer would do the opposite.

The reader would think they were reading about two entirely different characters. Which one should they believe? They would probably opt for the one that best suits their prejudices.

If you can do this to a recent figure, who most of us remember vividly and independently of any novelist or historian, imagine how much easier it is to do it to a figure who is distant in time, who we know nothing about apart from what the novelist or historian chooses to tell us?

Then we really taking them on trust. They may in fact be writing in all sincerity. But the point is that another writer could take the same set of basic data about the figure in question and interpret them very differently.

Things get even murkier when we try to guess the motives of someone for doing something. Was More dicing with death because he had a martyrdom complex or because he genuinely felt he could not sign the Oath of Supremacy? More himself questioned his own motives. We all question our own motives sometimes. Do we want something for selfish or unselfish reasons?

So when a writer tries to work out someone's motives, a lot of the time they are only guessing.

To sum up, approach *Wolf Hall* as a drama based on historical events and not as a true and accurate account of all the characters found therein because such an account is, in fact, impossible to obtain.

CHAPTER 62

WHY THE FEAST OF STEPHEN, THE FIRST CHRISTIAN MARTYR, IS SO APT THIS YEAR

2015

Today is St Stephen's Day, but I wonder how many people know anything about St Stephen, despite the fact that he has a day named after him?

St Stephen is mentioned in the Acts of the Apostles. Like all the early Christians, he was a Jewish convert. His skill at preaching quickly drew him to the attention of the religious authorities in Jerusalem. He was tried for blasphemy and stoned to death, making him the first Christian martyr. Since then, the number of Christians killed for their faith has soared into the millions. Sometimes they have been persecuted by other religions (and have persecuted those other religions in their turn).

Ancient Rome persecuted them because they would not recognise the Roman Emperor as a god and because they often made a convenient scapegoat when things were not going the empire's way.

The 20th Century was the worst in all history in terms of the numbers of Christians killed for their faith, usually by militantly atheistic regimes like those in the Soviet Union or China.

Today, the very worst country in terms of its suppression and persecution of religion is North Korea, which, like the old Soviet Union, is officially atheistic.

Shackles are also placed on religious freedom in other communist countries like China and Vietnam, and sometimes-religious believers are imprisoned, beaten up and even killed.

But today most of the worst attacks on Christians, and on members of other religious minorities as well, are taking place in Muslim countries, or areas with majority Muslim populations like northern Nigeria. Last week the Archbishop of Westminster, Cardinal Vincent Nichols, organised a meeting in London to draw attention to the persecution of Christians in the Middle East. Christian leaders from the region were present. The meeting was addressed by Prince Charles. Referring to 'Persecuted and Forgotten? A Report on Christians oppressed for their Faith 2013-15', by Aid to the Church in Need, he said: "The suffering [of Middle East Christians] is symptomatic of a very real crisis which threatens the very existence of Christians in the land of its birth."

By way of illustration, he added: "Christianity is on course to disappear from Iraq within five years, unless emergency help is provided on a greatly increased scale."

As we celebrate Christmas, it is sobering to think that last year, for the first time in 1,800 years, the birth of Christ could not be celebrated in Mosul, Iraq's second largest city. This is because in summer of last year, ISIS swept into Mosul and ordered the Christians out of the city. They fled to the relative safety of the Kurdish-controlled parts of Iraq or in some cases to Jordan. Irish Christians, and Christians in the West generally, are pitifully unaware of what is happening to their fellow believers in other parts of the world.

We celebrate Christmas because of events that took place in what was then Judea, what is now Israel and Palestine, 2,000 years ago.

Christianity grew first in that region and spread from there. Christianity became the major religion across the Middle East and North Africa until the Arab/Muslim conquests starting in the 7th Century. But through all the centuries since then, Christianity had managed to hang on as a minority religion in the Middle East. The Christians of the Middle East are of very ancient lineage. The Coptic Christians of Egypt are descended from the ancient Egyptians of pre-Arabic times.

The Christians of Northern Iraq are Assyrians and again long predate the Arab conquest. So when the Christians were driven from Mosul last year, so were the last of the Assyrians who have been in the region for thousands of years.

It is as if all Irish of Celtic descent were suddenly driven from this country. The Christians of Mosul would never have dreamt until a few years ago of the fate that has now befallen them.

A hundred years ago, Christians made up about 14% of the population of the Middle East. This is now put at 4%. Part of this decline is due to lower birth rates and natural emigration, but a very big part of it, especially in the last 10 years, is because the persecution of Christians in the Middle East has hugely intensified as militant Islam has grown in strength.

Last May, a Catholic Church delegation headed by Bishop John McAreavey appeared before the Joint Committee on Foreign Affairs and Trade to speak about the persecution of Christians in the Middle East. There needs to be much more of this in the coming year if the topic is to get the attention it deserves, if not in the national media, then at least among Christians on the island. It might seem strange to have the feast day of the first Christian martyr right after Christmas Day, with one day marking a birth and the next marking a death. But the juxtaposition isn't strange at all because Christians began to be killed for their faith from the very beginning of Christianity and Jesus himself was killed because of what he believed. So celebrating the two on successive days is actually completely apt and it is particularly apt this year because we are becoming witness to the fact that, because of persecution, Christianity is in danger of dying out in the part of the world where Christianity originated and where the event that we celebrate each Christmas took place.

To mark Christmas Day and St Stephen's Day one after the other is not just an act of memory, it is also an entirely fitting act of solidarity with those Christians who suffer and die today in huge numbers because of what they believe.

CHAPTER 63

A WORLD WITHOUT
DOWN'S SYNDROME IS TERRIFYING

2016

In Iceland, 100% of Down's Syndrome babies have been aborted every year for the last five years. This was only one of a number of very chilling revelations contained in a programme aired on BBC 2 last week called A World Without Down's Syndrome.

The programme was presented by comedienne and actress Sally Phillips, who is herself raising a Down's Syndrome child, her son Olly, aged 11. This obviously made the issue very personal for her. Her basic message was that thanks to ever more sophisticated pregnancy screening we are creating a world in which there may soon enough be no more Down's Syndrome children left.

At present, screening is 85% effective at detecting Down's Syndrome children in the womb. In her native Britain, 90% of detected Down's Syndrome babies are aborted, a colossal figure. This detection normally takes place at 20 plus weeks, meaning these abortions are quite late term. The babies are well developed at this point. No-one can call them a mere 'zygote' or those who defend their right to life 'zygopaths' as Fintan O'Toole did recently in an *Irish Times* column. (So much for 'calm and reasoned' debate on the issue.)

In another chilling moment on the programme, Phillips interviewed a woman who had her Down's Syndrome baby aborted at 25 weeks. The woman did not believe it was fair to bring a severely disabled child into the world. She described how she took a tablet to break down the placenta and then the doctors injected a solution into the baby that stopped its heart. This is the reality of abortion that pro-choice campaigners don't want us to hear about.

What was most chilling was the entirely matter-of-fact way in which the woman described how her baby was killed.

Phillips went on to discuss how a new screening technique is being rolled out and paid for out of public funds that will detect Down's Syndrome babies in the womb at around 12 weeks, not 20 weeks, and is 99% effective.

Phillips said this has already led to an increase in the number of Down's Syndrome babies being aborted. Here in Ireland, the Rotunda offers this new form of screening.

The Master of the Rotunda, Prof. Fergal Malone, says of it: "The advent of foetal DNA testing from the mother's blood is a major advance in screening, which has been available in Ireland for the past 12 months." This was in November 2014.

What Phillips found is that when women are told that their unborn babies have Down's Syndrome, doctors and nurses present them with a uniformly bleak picture of what this will mean both for the child and the rest of the family. They are presented with a list of the health problems Down's Syndrome children face. The child is seen as a burden only, as a burden to itself as well as to everyone else.

But to Sally Phillips her son Olly is a source of joy and Olly himself seems to be very joyful. Phillips spoke to a supporter of earlier screening of Down's Syndrome babies and this supporter seemed to think she had a killer argument (pun intended) when she asked Phillips what would happen to Olly once she had passed on.

Phillips, needless to say, believes society ought to have something better to offer than the mass aborting of such children.

A few weeks ago I wrote about the rise of eugenics, which means 'well born'. The belief of eugenics is that genetically imperfect children should not be born at all. Clearly this philosophy is now absolutely commonplace in society and, disastrously, in maternity services around the Western world.

The quest for 'genetic purity' is on, and the 'genetically impure' are being killed in vast numbers before they are born.

There was one weakness in Phillips' presentation, however. She is herself pro-choice. I suppose the BBC would never have allowed her to make the programme if she was anything else and I guess the British public would simply have dismissed her out of hand if she was not for legalised abortion.

But this only shows what happens when a society has normalised abortion to the extent that Britain has. You won't even get a hearing unless you are in some way, shape or form in favour of abortion.

Phillips, who came across in the programme as enormously likeable, would probably argue that while she is pro-choice she wishes that more people would make the choice not to abort Down's Syndrome babies.

She argues that when a woman is told her child has Down's Syndrome she shouldn't be presented with a bleak picture only, she should also be presented with the many positive stories out there of people and families living with Down's Syndrome.

This would certainly be a big step in the right direction because eugenics has crept up on us almost unnoticed and now has society in an almost unbreakable lock grip.

Its logic is absolutely terrifying. If children deemed a 'burden' can be killed in the womb, if we are told it is for their own good, then why doesn't this logic apply after they are born? In fact, it does apply, and fully.

We see it in the way assisted suicide is gaining a hold on Western societies. In Belgium, children living lives of "unbearable suffering" can now offer themselves for assisted suicide.

The inescapable fact is that abortion makes lives dispensable, and not just the lives of the 'genetically imperfect' although it bears down on them most severely. In the end it makes all 'imperfect lives', or 'inconvenient lives' dispensable in the name of 'choice'.

When St John Paul II coined the expression 'culture of death' this is exactly what he was talking about. The situation is growing ever worse and ever more inhumane.

CHAPTER 64

HUMAN RIGHTS BEGAN WITH CHRIST'S HUMBLE BIRTH

2016

Even if you view Jesus Christ simply as a human being, not the Word Incarnate, on Christmas Day we still celebrate one of the most epochal events in world history; his birth. However you look it at, the birth of this man was the start of an immense, culture-changing series of events that have resonated through history, and in almost all parts of the world down to the present day.

That it should have been the birth of a man in very humble circumstances, to a humble family in an obscure part of the Roman Empire that started this sequence of events only makes it more remarkable.

It is more remarkable still when we consider that he was executed by the Romans. Even if you take the Dan Brown view that Jesus disappeared off to the South of France with Mary Magdalene where he died a natural death in old age, it is still remarkable that his life led to the founding of such a world-shaping religion.

Indeed, if he did not die and rise again, the fact that his disciples, at huge risk to their own lives, nonetheless took it upon themselves to spread his message, takes on yet more improbable dimensions.

Christianity is built first and foremost on the belief that we ought to follow Jesus, to be his disciples, to strive to be like him. The Church is the community of those who share this goal. This is at the heart of Christianity.

˧   But Christianity was also the first universal creed. The Christian message was not simply for a particular family, or clan or tribe or people, but for all peoples everywhere and at all times. Liberal internationalism, which is also universal in aspiration, is a direct descendant of Christian universalism. Before Christianity, in the West at any rate, it didn't occur to anyone that a given set of religious beliefs was for everyone.

There, of course, lies one of the sources of criticism of Christianity, that it wants to bring everyone into its house and it has sometimes done terrible things to this end. The same criticism applies to liberal internationalism.

Although Christ is first and foremost at the heart of Christianity, so is something else, an immense and far-reaching moral doctrine, and this is the belief that we are all created morally equal.

If you have the slightest interest in intellectual history, then can I suggest you read *Inventing the Individual: the Origins of Western Liberalism* by Larry Siedentop, a former Fellow of Keble College, Oxford? Mr Siedentop is secular and liberal but recognises the enormous debt Western civilisation owes to Christianity and how modern liberalism has grown out of Christianity.

He shows that prior to Christianity, the belief that we are all created morally equal did not exist. Instead, the widespread belief was that your moral status and your social status were inextricably linked.

Christianity, on the other hand, introduced the belief that no matter how low or how high your social station, morally we are all absolutely equal in the sight of God, so that the peasant at his plough is the moral equal of the Emperor in Rome, or the Pope in Rome for that matter.

Commenting on the finding of a survey that fewer than half of Britons now consider themselves to be Christian, the *Guardian* leader writer worried that if Christianity was ever to fade from view completely, so would one of the foundation stones of human rights, namely this belief that we are all created morally equal.

The leader writer said: "The idea that people have some rights just because they are human, and entirely irrespective of merit, certainly isn't derived from observation of the world. It arose out of Christianity, no matter how much Christians have in practice resisted it. Although human rights have become embedded in our institutions at the same time as religious observance has been in decline, they could become vulnerable in an entirely post-Christian environment where the collective memory slips from the old moorings inherited from Christian ethics."

The *Guardian* is a frequent critic of Christianity. Its outlook is left-wing and secular, but it could still print an editorial like this.

The leader writer was under no illusions about the fact that the Church itself has often been the enemy of its own belief that we are all morally equal. Why was this? The reason is that it often formed alliances with the 'principalities and powers' of the day and therefore often ended up doing their bidding instead of following the Gospel. This is why the Enlightenment, whose own legacy is ambiguous, was necessary.

But the *Guardian's* leader writer is realistic enough to see that the belief that we are all bearers of rights, irrespective of merit, simply because we are human, "arose out of Christianity".

That is to say, it is a Christian doctrine just as the belief that Jesus rose from the dead is a Christian doctrine.

Christianity teaches we are morally equal because we all are made in the image and likeness of God. If we are instead the accidental by-products of blind evolution, why should we be morally equal? The universe itself confers no worth whatever on us, any more than it confers worth on a stone.

So, it is undeniable that the birth of Christ was epoch-making. It was more epoch-making than many people today realise. Many of the beliefs we take for granted, including our belief in human rights, owe more to Christianity than most of us today suspect.

And this, of course, is without considering the vastly bigger claim; that Jesus was indeed God-made man. If that is true, then his birth could not possibly have been more epochal.

CHAPTER 65

WHEN 'POLITICAL CORRECTNESS' CAN'T BULLY ANYMORE

2016

What happens to political correctness when its ability to bully everyone into silence comes to an end? Donald Trump 2016 US election victory signals that it is coming to an end. Strange as it may seem for someone like me to say, however, if it came to a complete end, that would be a bad thing because the basic instinct of political correctness is good: protect minorities.

The problem with political correctness is that it has completely over-reached. By shouting 'bigot' too often, by completely failing to distinguish between reasonable and unreasonable critics, it is getting closer to wearing out the power of the word 'bigot'. It's not there yet by any means, but give it a few more years.

In addition, in its eagerness to protect minorities, it has covered up some terrible abuses perpetrated by those same minorities, including sexual abuse (just like the Church did), and voter fraud.

Mr Trump basically set out to defy almost all the conventions of po-litical correctness. He turned its censoriousness to his own advantage. He seemed to know that the more politically incorrect he was, the more pub-licity he would attract. He also seemed to sense that because political cor-rectness can't distinguish between reasonable and unreasonable criticism, and shouts 'bigot' at absolutely everyone, he might as well be hanged for a sheep as for a lamb.

That's what happens when you impose the 'death penalty' for all of-fences. You tempt some people to commit a big offence.

Lots of people who wouldn't agree with some of Mr Trump's more out-rageous statements - for example, ban all Muslims (later nuanced to 'vet Muslims') - still voted for him because they were sick and tired of being shouted down all the time. Mr Trump might be a barbarian, a club-wielding caveman, but maybe it took someone like him, instead of the more polite critics of political correctness, to deliver a mighty blow to it.

The danger here in Ireland is that the shrill and unthinking defenders of political correctness will in time give rise to a similar, home-grown version of Mr Trump because nothing else seems to get through to them.

They are impervious to reason, assume the bad faith of everyone they disagree with and go from zero to total denunciation in the time it takes you to blink.

I wish there was a term better than 'political correctness' to describe 'political correctness'. I could say 'cultural Marxism' but almost no one would know what that means.

As mentioned, political correctness is concerned with protecting the rights and status of minority groups. The reason it is so concerned with language is that the wrong kind of language can demean a group. That is why 'tinker' changed to 'itinerant' and then to 'traveller', for example. We won't even mention the 'k' word.

Nor will we mention the 'n' word, for very obvious reasons, but even good-willed people aren't sure whether to say 'black' or 'African-American'. There is no organisation called 'African-American Lives Matter'. It's 'Black Lives Matter'. So, can it really be racist to say 'black'?

We should sometimes have to think twice about some of the language we use to describe this or that group. The trouble is that political correctness has us thinking three, four, ten times about the language we use and has reached the absurdity of seeking to make us fear whether it is safe to call a man a man or a woman a woman in case the person prefers some gender-neutral term. And if you don't use the right term, you are, of course, a 'bigot'.

In 2016, Health Minister Simon Harris wrote a ridiculous defence of political correctness and warned us to be 'afraid' of anyone who warns that it has gone too far. At the time, I gave some examples of it doing precisely that, for example, 'safe spaces' and 'no platforming' at universities, so-called 'anti-hate' laws, the shutting down generally of one debate about another through scaring people rigid in case they say the 'wrong' thing.

I ought to have given some even worse examples; for instance, what happened in British towns like Rotherham, Rochdale and Oxford. In those places, Pakistani men were guilty of sexually assaulting and raping hundreds of girls, often underage, over a series of years but the whole thing was covered up by the local authorities, including politicians, in case the revelation incited racism.

Similarly, when 'men of North African appearance' sexually assaulted women in the centre of Cologne and elsewhere on New Year's Eve last, the German police initially covered it up. It came out on social media and the dreaded Breitbart website. In Tower Hamlets in London, meanwhile, voter fraud was covered up because, again, those responsible were from a racial minority.

You won't have heard of Nissar Hussain, who has been subjected to brutal assault and had to be moved to a safe house by the British police within the last week. Why was he so moved? Because he is a Muslim convert to Christianity. Why haven't we heard of him? Because his assailants are Muslims.

When political correctness is crushing free speech, and covering up sex assault, physical assault and voter fraud, that should absolutely scream that it has gone too far, that its anxiety to protect minorities has spun completely and dangerously out of control.

The topic, 'has political correctness gone too far?' has never been properly debated in the Irish media because, presumably, such a discussion would itself be politically incorrect. The more we stifle debate, however, the more people are condemned for saying reasonable things that defy the PC orthodoxies, the more we see terrible human rights abuses covered up in the name of those orthodoxies, the more likely it is that we will have more Donald Trumps.

For the sake of civility, we need a mild form of political correctness, but the totally virulent form of it currently on the loose threatens to destroy it completely.

CHAPTER 66

TRUE BELIEVERS IN SPORT OR RELIGION DON'T WALK AWAY DUE TO SCANDALS

2016

The Olympic games and the Catholic Church are two institutions beset by scandals of one sort or another.

Sport in general has been engulfed by numerous different kinds of scandals. The question is whether those of us who are 'true believers' - whether in sport or in the Catholic Church, or both - keep faith in them or turn away disillusioned? I'm for keeping faith, but reforming where and when necessary.

The first really big doping scandal occurred at the 1988 games in Seoul, South Korea, after Ben Johnson had blitzed the field in the 100m final. He was subsequently found to be a cheat on a grand scale. Since then, one sprinter after another has been found to be using performance-enhancing drugs and served temporary bans. Plenty of these have been Americans.

Back in the days of the Eastern bloc, we all rightly suspected that athletes from East Germany and elsewhere were also cheating on a grand scale. The performances in the women's sports in particular, whether track and field or in the pool, seemed too good to be true, and were. Some of the records set in the 1980s stood for decades afterwards.

Now we have heard even of African athletes who have cheated. That really was a blow, because the success of African athletes, often from desperately poor countries, especially in the middle and long distance events, seemed to harken back to the days of amateur sport and the Corinthian ideal.

Add all of this together and it explains why the Olympics don't generate anything like the excitement they once did. We can't be certain about what we're watching anymore. Are we watching a clean win, or a tainted one? It's a disaster for the athletes who are clean.

Of course, the Olympics are not alone in being affected by drugs scandals. Cycling has had plenty as well and Arsenal football manager, Arsene Wenger, doesn't think the problem is being pursued with sufficient vigour by the authorities in his sport.

All sports have been affected by betting scandals, including boxing, football and tennis. Tennis is only the latest to have been engulfed in a betting scandal and we just recently saw Maria Sharapova suspended for using a banned substance.

There have also been sex scandals in sport. College football is huge in America and the coach of Pennsylvania State football team was convicted a few years ago of multiple counts of child abuse. Some officials from Penn State were accused of engaging in a cover-up.

Here in Ireland, we have seen sex abuse scandals involving children in the likes of boxing and swimming.

This brings us on to the Catholic Church, the reputation of which has been enormously damaged by child sex abuse scandals made much worse by the cover-ups. What is reportedly happening at Maynooth is of a different, lesser order compared with this, but it hardly inspires confidence. Persistent reports of sexually inappropriate behaviour down the years by a small minority of students are not going to attract vocations.

This is separate from the question of what exactly should be taught at a seminary and what kind of spiritual formation should be received. A false dichotomy has been created between 'pastoral' priests on the one hand, and 'doctrinally rigid' priests on the other. It is possible to be pastoral and orthodox, and to be liberal and have poor people skills.

I suspect a young Karol Wojtyla or Joseph Ratzinger (the future John Paul II and Benedict XVI respectively) would not have made it into some seminaries today. They would be deemed too 'rigid' because of their orthodoxy despite the fact that Fr Wojtyla was an excellent parish priest and Joseph Ratzinger was considered one of the most approachable lecturers when he worked at a university in his native Germany.

Why do people believe in sport? It's because we like competition, and competition at its best breeds excellence. But we don't stop playing football (say) or watching football because we're annoyed at the scandals in world football's governing body, FIFA. We continue to support football because we believe in football itself.

Tremendous numbers of people have had their lives transformed for the better by sport and tremendous numbers of us take great pleasure from sport. If we believe in it, we can't abandon it. Instead we have to reform it.

The same goes for religion. Religion, despite all the charges that can be made against it, has also transformed countless lives for the better down the ages as countless numbers of people can personally testify. There is also the not-so trivial matter that for religious believers, God is real and nothing is ultimately more important than that ultimate fact. The vast majority of people in all ages have believed in God or gods because we are religious by nature, and even when we are not explicitly religious we find substitutes, like various ideologies, or, in point of fact, sport itself, which can inspire religious-like fervour.

So those who believe in the Catholic Church, or some other branch of Christianity, or in some other religion, cannot walk away when these have problems any more than someone who loves a given sport will stop playing it or following it because of corruption and other scandals. Instead you work to make things better. That's why I don't walk away from the Church, or from sport for that matter. You don't walk away if you believe in the thing in itself.

CHAPTER 67

FRANCIS SEEKS TO AVOID THE ERRORS OF BOTH 'LIBERALS' AND 'CONSERVATIVES'

2016

The very first Christians lived in a world that was alien to their values. One way in which it was alien was in its attitude to divorce. Both Jewish society, from which the first Christians emerged, and the Roman society in which Christianity took root, allowed divorce and remarriage. Men in particular could discard an unwanted wife very easily.

Christianity took a very strict view. Following the words of Christ, marriage was to be permanent and indissoluble. Some Christians allowed for some exceptions to this rule, but Christianity has never been lenient about divorce.

The early Christians could easily have accommodated themselves and their nascent Church to the mores they saw around them with respect to divorce. They could have concluded that they would make no progress in converting people to Christianity unless they adapted Christ's teaching. But they didn't do this. Instead, they adapted the culture.

This arose from self-confidence. They believed in what they were doing.

The Church today does not have this strong self-confidence. It doubts itself. I am not just referring here to the Catholic Church, but to Christianity more broadly.

Like the early Christians, the Church today finds itself in a society that readily accepts divorce, but unlike those early Christians it has lost faith in its ability to convert society to its view. It doubts this view itself.

It is worried it is losing people because of the growing disconnect between how we live now and what Christianity teaches.

Various branches of Christianity have approached this problem in different ways. The liberal Churches have adapted. This goes to the extremes of the Lutherans in Sweden where a senior Lutheran bishop has said he favours abortion rights. Divorce has long since been accepted.

This has not brought Swedes back to church. All it has done is drive away the orthodox faithful who have not been replaced.

The Catholic Church has taken the view that it must hold fast to what it believes are eternal truths and the teachings handed down by Christ. To do otherwise would be a huge act of infidelity, and even on pragmatic terms would not work given the massive failure of the liberal Protestant approach.

Under Pope Francis, the Catholic Church continues to teach what it has always believed to be true on all the important issues. Last week saw the release of a new papal document called *Amoris Laetitia* (The Joy of Love). It is the most important document of his papacy to date.

Abortion, in the eyes of the Church, is as categorically wrong as it ever was.

About gay marriage, the Pope says: "There are absolutely no grounds for considering homosexual unions to be in any way similar or even remotely analogous to God's plan for marriage and family."

Surrogacy is "the exploitation and commercialisation of the female body".

Gender ideology denies "the difference and reciprocity in nature of a man and a woman and envisages a society without sexual differences, thereby eliminating the anthropological basis of the family".

And so on.

So where is the friendly, smiling, accommodating Pope Francis in this? He is still very much there. Pope Francis was never going to change the fundamental teachings of Catholicism. As he has said, 'I am a son of the Church'.

What he has an absolute horror of, however, is a type of Christianity that uses the teachings of the Church simply as an opportunity to judge and condemn people.

This is the Christianity that will say to the cohabiting couple, 'I condemn you. Go away until you mend your ways'. Likewise, with the person who is divorced and remarried, or who has had a child outside of marriage.

Quite apart from the scandals, it is the harsh and authoritarian presentation of its teachings that has alienated untold numbers of people from the Church.

Francis is therefore telling the Church and its pastors to adopt a wholly different approach. The cohabiting couple should not be condemned and sent away. Nor should the person who is divorced and remarried. Nor should the woman who has had a child outside of marriage.

Instead the Church should look first for the good in the lives of people. The cohabiting couple, for example, might have a very strong, loving relationship, better than what many married couples have.

There is a key passage in Amoris Laetitia that really sums up his whole pastoral outlook. Referring to "irregular situations", Pope Francis says: "There are two ways of thinking which occur throughout the Church's history: casting off and reinstating. The Church's way, from the time of the Council of Jerusalem [in the first Century] has always been the way of Jesus, the way of mercy and reinstatement [in the Church]."

He says: "No one can be condemned forever, because that is not the logic of the Gospel." Here he has in mind in particular the divorced and remarried.

But elsewhere he states: "In order to avoid all misunderstanding, I would point out that in no way must the Church desist from proposing the full ideal of marriage, God's plan in all its grandeur."

He says: "A lukewarm attitude, any kind of relativism, or an undue reticence in proposing that ideal, would be a lack of fidelity to the Gospel and also of love on the part of the Church for young people themselves."

Within the Church, as in society, conservatives are concerned to uphold certain moral standards, and this can easily harden into the sort of harsh authoritarianism that the Pope rightly condemns.

But liberalism easily becomes the opposite error. A liberal pastor who meets a cohabiting couple certainly won't condemn them, but he might very well never encourage them to marry either if they seem happy as they are. He might adopt an 'I'm ok, you're ok' approach.

This kind of error is much more prevalent in the Church today, in the West at least, than the opposite error.

In fact, any priest who believes Pope Francis has effectively given him permission to play down the Church's teachings on marriage and the family has simply not been listening to what he is really saying.

Pope Francis does not want the Church's teachings to be used as a stick to beat people with, but he does want them to be offered to people in their fullness, and for people to be encouraged, bit by bit if need be, to live them out in their fullness. Anything else betrays what Pope Francis is really driving at.

CHAPTER 68

PRESIDENT HIGGINS USES HIS OFFICE AS A LEFT-WING PULPIT – AND THE MEDIA LETS HIM

2016

In a speech delivered at an event in Dublin's Mansion House in 2016 called 'Remembering 1916', President Michael D. Higgins warned his audience of the risk that a "commemoration might be exploited for partisan purposes". Having rightly delivered that warning, he then plunged on and became deeply partisan in his own 'remembering' of 1916.

This has been his wont since assuming the office of President in 2011.

His intention in his speech, he declared, was an "appraisal of Irish nationalism from the point of view of the egalitarian tradition which manifested itself before and during the Easter Rising, but which was progressively and, I should argue, consciously, repressed over the subsequent decades".

He asked, "Why and how has the flame of equality and social justice been quenched?"

He approvingly noted that the programme of the First Dáil was "powerfully egalitarian" and was "linked to an international movement that was pushing a great change towards a socialist vision of politics, economy and society..."

President Higgins then outlined the ways in which this vision had been frustrated by conservative elements in Irish society, causing it to collapse into a "property-driven conservatism... the fetishisation of land and private property, a restrictive religiosity and a repressive pursuit of respectability".

He invited his audience, and us, to reclaim "the joy of making equality the central theme of our Republic".

This is partisan. This is favouring one particular political tradition over others. How could he warn us against making the commemoration of 1916 partisan in one part of his speech, and then do this? Could he not see the contradiction?

Two days before we had similar stuff from his wife, Sabina, in a speech delivered at the graveside of Countess Markievicz.

There is a "new form of capitalism", she said, "that seeks to undermine democracy itself". There are "empires of greed", which are "even more powerful and unaccountable" than the empire that the rebels of 1916 had to contend with.

This is simply more evidence that the President and his wife between them have turned the presidency into a pulpit for a left-wing point of view. The presidency was never designed to be a pulpit for any ideological point of view, whether right or left wing. It is supposed to be above politics, and therefore uniting.

The only way Michael D gets away with this is because he has the backing of most of the media, and because the political parties have been content to let him at it. In addition, academia in Ireland, as elsewhere, is almost entirely left-wing, and therefore it is happy for him to use the Presidency to trumpet its point of view.

Imagine, however, if instead of having President Michael D. Higgins in office we had President Michael McDowell instead, or, Heaven forbid, President Dana Rosemary Scallon. Imagine if McDowell used the office to laud the benefits of free markets, and imagine if Dana used it to laud the virtues of Catholicism.

We don't have to imagine very hard. There would be uproar. But if it is acceptable for Michael D. Higgins to use the office to promote his left-wing views, then why would it be unacceptable for a McDowell or a Dana to use the office to promote their views? Now that the office has been so politicised, what objection can there be in principle to any future president doing such a thing?

It is no good Michael D. objecting that he was elected with a million votes (700,000 first-preference votes, actually). The point is that once you surrender the principle that the presidency should be above politics, you can hardly complain when someone uses the office to promote an ideology you don't like.

The fact that Higgins' ideological vision as outlined in his Mansion House address, and many other similar addresses since he became president, demands a response in kind simply proves the extent to which he has politicised the presidency. No one should have to argue against the President of Ireland's weirdly ahistorical view of 1916 and subsequent developments, or his totally crude and simplistic caricature of capitalism. No one should have to argue against them because he should have left these views at the door of his office when elected President.

But seeing as he has not done that, let's argue against them. Let's attend to his ahistorical view of 1916 and subsequent developments first. In his Mansion House speech, he almost totally glosses over the fact that many of our leaders from 1917 on were rightly and profoundly worried by the socialist vision that was then newly on offer in the Soviet Union.

That vision was not restricted to the Soviet Union. It was enthusiastically shared by socialists everywhere. It was absolutely prudent for our political leadership a hundred years ago to worry that our home-grown socialists had a similar vision in mind for Ireland.

We should, in fact, be extremely thankful that Ireland did not adopt either of the two totalitarian ideologies then coming into vogue on the continent, namely communism and fascism. This was a democratic State from the get-go, flawed in many ways, but democratic. That is something to be proud of in the context of the early to mid-20th Century.

As for his critique of capitalism, in the imaginings of Michael D. Higgins, it was through the work of socialists like him that the poor were lifted up from their squalor and given jobs and a standard of living that people could only have dreamt of in 1916.

But none of this would have been possible without economic growth - and that growth was delivered by free markets and free trade, both of which were, and are, vigorously opposed by socialism.

In fact, it was only when this country shook off its protectionist economic policies (supported both by de Valera and by the left) and embraced free trade that the country began to prosper at all.

There is much more to be written on this point. Suffice it to say that if the country had espoused the vision a hundred years ago that President

Higgins lauds today, we would be far worse off than we are. This, after all, is a man who never came across a revolutionary movement he did not like, such as the revolution the late Hugo Chavez inflicted on Venezuela.

Chavez led Venezuela to a level of economic disaster far beyond anything this country has experienced, and that was not because of the machinations of evil capitalists, but because of the inherent flaws of his economic programme. Some vision.

CHAPTER 69

HARSH VICTORIAN MORALITY AT CORE OF MOTHER AND BABY HOME SCANDALS

2017

Attitudes to unmarried mothers and their babies have changed back and forth over the centuries. The historian Ivy Pinchbeck says that in medieval England, children born outside of marriage were not viewed as being as much of a problem as later; they were absorbed into their mothers' communities and worked on the farms like everyone else.

From Elizabethan times, with the introduction of the first Poor Laws, attitudes began to harden, and then hardened again in the 19th Century in both Britain and Ireland. An award-winning essay by Dorothy L. Haller called *Bastardy and Baby Farming in Victorian England* shows how society's attitude became even more punitive in the 19th Century and this legacy continued well into the 20th Century, with only some attempts to soften the edges.

Ms Haller writes that prior to the 1830s, unmarried mothers and their babies tended to be looked after reluctantly, out of parish funds, but then it was decided they were too much of a drain on scarce parish resources. They were to be dealt with under new Poor Laws that made it even harder for them to receive help, including from the father of the child.

Previously the father could sometimes be forced to pay for the upkeep of his child, but it was decided by the chancellor of the day that forcing men to pay for their 'illegitimate' children made them "victims of the seducer's art".

The hardening of attitudes to unmarried mothers seems to have happened almost across the board. Many Christians supported it, but so did followers of the rising philosophy of utilitarianism, who were often not at all religious, and who tended to believe in the doctrine of the 'survival of the fittest'.

The Gradgrind character in Charles Dickens' *Hard Times* caricatures the type.

The new Poor Law of 1834 led to the widespread establishment of workhouses and so on. Unmarried mothers and their babies now found the world an even harsher place.

The Times of London declared in 1834 that relief to mothers of 'illegitimate' children had reached "a pitch extremely oppressive to the parishes, and grievously detrimental to female morals".

There were lots more of this kind of thing from the leading organs and thinkers of the day and it lasted for decades. A distinction between the deserving and undeserving poor was made very clear. This was Victorian morality writ large.

The laws and the institutions developed under this new, harsher dispensation for unmarried mothers and their children extended to Ireland. Here, as in England, the churches ran many of the institutions.

After we won independence in 1922, the Catholic Church and Irish society, instead of looking at the system of institutions we inherited and radically reforming, if not abolishing and replacing them, seemed to instead double down on the worst kind of Victorian morality.

This is what helps to explain the Tuam Mother and Baby home, and other similar institutions in this country and elsewhere. (Mother and baby homes continued to exist in Britain until well after the middle of the last century.)

Enda Kenny spoke about the matter in the Dáil in 2017.

He said: "Tuam is not just a burial ground, it is a social and cultural sepulchre. That is what it is. As a society in the so-called 'good old days', we did not just hide away the dead bodies of tiny human beings, we dug deep and deeper still to bury our compassion, our mercy and our humanity itself. No nuns broke into our homes to kidnap our children. We gave them up to what we convinced ourselves was the nuns' care."

His tone and his words contrasted very sharply with those of Labour's Kathleen Lynch in 2013 when she addressed the Dáil about Bethany Home, which also housed unmarried mothers and their babies.

Ms Lynch, then the junior minister in the Department of Justice, used much softer language than the Taoiseach, even though hundreds of babies also died in Bethany Home and were buried in an unmarked grave.

Explaining the high death rate in the Protestant-run institution she said: "Unfortunately, poverty and disease were commonplace in Ireland up to the 1950s and this was reflected in infant mortality rates.

"Infant mortality rates in the 1940s were at a level that is hard to comprehend today, about 20 times higher than now and that figure applies across the entire population. For those who were malnourished and subject to disease and a lack of hygiene, the figures would have been higher still."

Responding to critics of the home, she said: "Our Constitution demands we respect the rules of natural justice. People are entitled to a fair hearing and an opportunity to protect their good name... it seems to have been accepted at the time that Bethany Home was run by people with charitable motives."

Was Ms Lynch's speech about the Bethany Home too soft? Did Mr Kenny's speech get the tone right?

I hope the commission set up to investigate our mother and baby homes and the county homes gets to the bottom of what exactly happened to those babies and their mothers. I hope it throws a full light on why they were established and how they were run.

I hope it finds out exactly why infant mortality rates were so high in them. I hope it finds out why the bodies were often put in unmarked graves and what the burial practices were for the very poor in those decades.

I hope it looks at what was happening before the mother and baby homes came into existence and what were the realistic alternatives to them.

I hope it looks at what was happening in other countries. For example, in social democratic Sweden, where they were sterilising unmarried mothers.

I hope it gives us a full and complete understanding of the whole miserable business and that this will help deliver both truth and justice. Nothing less will do.

CHAPTER 70

BREXIT: A REBELLION BY 'PEOPLE OF SOMEWHERE' AGAINST 'ANYWHERE'

2017

For a very brief period after the 2016 election of Donald Trump - it lasted for about a nanosecond - the liberal establishment paused to reflect on whether it had lost touch with a big portion of the electorate.

It was decided, in this all-too-brief moment, that the concerns of blue-collar voters had not been sufficiently listened to, and that there was a backlash against the tightening strictures of political correctness.

But then it was swiftly back to wild condemnations of 'bigots', and 'white supremacists' and so on. Large segments of the electorate were declared anathema.

The reaction to Brexit has been the same. After a very brief period of reflection, it was back to outright condemnation.

The left, the soft left at any rate, found itself in the very strange position of being against vast swathes of working-class voters. The soft left was more concerned with advancing globalisation and immigration and multiculturalism than with protecting the real and perceived interests of the working class.

Here in Ireland we took a smug pleasure in the thought that we would never do something as stupid as withdraw from the European Union. In the minds of its most ardent supporters, the EU is a shining city on the hill, one that bares little enough resemblance to its far more mundane and often undemocratic reality.

Towards the end of Britain's EU referendum, there were demonstrations by Remainers urging people to vote for 'love, not hate'. This is the sort of utterly reductionist way in which many liberals now view politics. You are either on their side, the side of 'love', or on the side of 'hate'.

This kind of appalling analysis is making modern politics increasingly sectarian in character.

Let's return now to trying to properly understand why someone would vote for Brexit, or indeed for Mr Trump.

A good place to start is with a new book called *The Road to Somewhere: the Populist Revolt and the Future of Politics* by British intellectual David Goodhart.

Mr Goodhart is an interesting character. He founded, and for a number of years edited, the centre-left magazine *Prospect*. He now describes himself as a "post-liberal". He has switched allegiances to those who prefer the local over the global.

He characterises the new political divide as being between those who identify with 'anywhere', and those who identify with 'somewhere'.

The people from 'anywhere' are the globalised elite and those who identify with them are typically middle class, university educated and living in big cities.

They are all for multiculturalism, the EU, the UN, and they don't identify strongly with local communities and traditions because they believe these are the incubators of bigotry. They would be happy to live anywhere that shares their values. New York is more or less the same to them as London.

The people from 'somewhere' identify most strongly with the places most familiar to them, the places where they have roots and where there are established patterns of life they like.

These people tend to be rural or working class.

The people from 'somewhere' are barely represented by mainstream politics anymore and are treated with the utmost contempt. Mainstream politics is completely dominated by the people from 'anywhere' who advance their own interests and concerns above all.

In the US, the people from 'somewhere' rose up in rebellion by voting for Mr Trump, often in full knowledge of how deeply unappealing he is but also in full knowledge that voting for him was a way of hitting out at the people who have treated them with such scorn for years.

In Britain, the people from 'somewhere' voted for Brexit. They know that the EU is run by people who don't really care about the effects of globalisation and immigration and multiculturalism on local communities and familiar patterns. The people from 'somewhere' don't like when the familiar becomes unfamiliar and don't appreciate being called 'bigots' for preferring what's closest to them.

In Ireland, oddly enough, the people from 'somewhere' have barely made their voices heard. Maybe this is because, fisheries aside, we didn't really have any big industries that were hurt by globalisation and because the type of immigration we have had to date hasn't made large parts of our country seem unfamiliar to us.

Like it or not, however, we are being affected by the rebellion of the 'somewhere people' because of Brexit, and if the 'anywhere people' continue to ignore their concerns, the rebellion is going to be a long-term feature of modern politics. In other words, get used to it and try to understand it.